HENRY JENKINS ROBERT V. KOZINETS

BOOK 2:

FANDOM AS AUDIENCE

in the Frames of Fandom Series

GATEWAY
PLANET PRESS

Founded in 2024, Gateway Planet Press is committed to publishing innovative and useful knowledge that reaches beyond the confines of traditional academic presses. Our mission is to deliver accessible, affordable, and high-quality research and teaching resources to scholars, professionals, and curious readers worldwide. By embracing new technologies and fresh perspectives, we seek to foster understanding, inspire critical thought, and, where necessary, spark meaningful change. This is just the beginning. Many journeys are possible—let us be your gateway.

Gateway Planet Press

Los Angeles, California

Fandom as Audience: Book 2 in the Frames of Fandom Series was
Edited by Samuel Boyce Miles
Formatted by Dawn Black
Indexed by Henry Jenkins and Robert V. Kozinets
Cover Designed by Robert V. Kozinets and Henry Jenkins from a photo by Henry Jenkins

Final Cover Art by Robert V. Kozinets

ISBN: 979-8-9992083-0-9

FRAMES OF FANDOM:
The Book Series

TABLE OF CONTENTS

PREFACE:
Welcome to Book Two

Gone are the days when fandoms were relegated to the fringes of pop culture. Nowadays, fandoms are thriving, woven into the webwork of our collective conversation and experiences, profoundly interlinked with our identities, and influencing our decision-making. They encompass not only sports and entertainment franchises but also a full spectrum of activities and interests that engage diverse, passionate audiences.

Welcome, Gentle Reader, to this book, **Fandom as Audience**, the second in a series exploring the multifarious world of fandom. Throughout these books, we examine, explain, and find delight in these diverse and varied manifestations of fans and fandoms. To understand them, we adopt a series of different conceptual perspectives, viewpoints, or frames.

This book is one volume in a 15-book series called **Frames of Fandom**. Each book is self-contained; they can be read separately or in any order. If you choose to read them in sequence, you will find there is an intentional logic and flow, which makes it the optimal experience. We briefly considered releasing them as an episodic book series reminiscent of the serial formats of the original fan tales, like

Sherlock Holmes or Batman. However, this notion was disregarded in favor of a series that presented a collection of stories and conceptual connections that try to bring to life the captivating world of fandoms that would then be explained using the most sophisticated frameworks currently available. This is done by using a series of frames (ways of understanding) that each represents a lens through which to consider what kind of community a fandom is and how it relates to the popular culture it consumes. We celebrate the collectives that have emerged, the impact they wield, and the potential they hold for business and society.

When you see a bolded title, such as **Fandom as Subculture** or **Locations of Fandom**, this is meant to signify the title of a book in the series, or the series itself. Throughout this book and the others, we will be referring to these books as if they are all already published. Because we are publishing them on a staggered schedule over a period of time, not all of the books we refer to may yet be available; however, they have all been written at the time of this release. Eventually, we will have all of the books we mentioned available to you, and this book will be an accurate reflection of the entire series.

Each book in **Frames of Fandom** focuses on a particular framework or paradigm that scholars have used to understand some of the complex dimensions of fandom. These frames may overlap, as in the case of **Fandom as Co-Creation** or **Fandom as Participatory Culture**. Both explain fandom as a site of cultural production, the first from the perspective of the media industry and within the field of consumer research, and the second from the perspective of the fan and within the theoretical traditions of cultural studies. Sometimes, one frame, say, **Fandom as Public**, provides the preconditions for the second, **Fandom as Activism**. In some cases, the relationship between the two is harder to define, such as the focus on affect in **Fandom as Desire** and on religion in **Fandom as Devotion.** Nevertheless, however encyclopedic the scope of this project may seem, the range of frames here is not exhaustive. We do, however, try to capture the majority of the dominant paradigms in the field.

Fandom as Audience, this second book in the series, traces the historical and conceptual journey of fandom from traditional audience studies to the field of fandom studies. Beginning with the conception of audiences as spectatorial observers shaped by demographic categories, it traces the evolution of fandom up to the mid-20th century, when marketers, media producers, and researchers began to recognize the importance of segmentation and targeting. This realization that fan audiences could be treated as markets with distinct psychographic profiles and cultural investments laid the groundwork for a new understanding of media consumption. In the early chapters, we explore how this commercial interest intersected with theoretical developments, particularly Raymond Williams' notion that culture is "ordinary," shaped by everyday life and intersecting identities rather than confined to elite spaces.

As the book progresses, it introduces and extends Stuart Hall's encoding/decoding model of audience interpretation. Hall's insights give rise to the core theme of audience agency, which underpins much of this book's analysis. It then explores the historical transition from audience studies to fandom studies, marking a turning point where the study of science fiction and popular culture audiences became a vehicle for understanding the participatory nature of fan communities. Through case studies ranging from the television series *Dallas* to Bollywood, we present the global diversity of audiences and how they integrate media texts into their local cultural contexts. The book also delves into the complexities of fandom, examining how fans ultimately influence media production itself in transmedia environments. Through a synthesis of theory, case studies, and cultural analysis, **Fandom as Audience** demonstrates that the media audience is not a static entity; it is a fluid, culturally embedded collective with the power to shape, resist, and co-create meaning alongside and within the work of media producers.

Goals of this Book Series

As we embark on our exploration into the frames of fandom, please keep in mind that we do so with three purposes. The first is intellectual. This book series seeks to develop the synergies between Henry's world of fandom studies and Rob's world of marketing and consumer research. For those wondering who the eponymous Henry and Rob are, it's us: Henry Jenkins and Robert Kozinets. Both of our native fields draw on tools and models from cultural anthropology to explain how ordinary people operate within a consumer economy in relation to the media industries. This stance would seem to provide common ground for us to learn from each other. In fact, we have been exchanging ideas with each other for almost 30 years.

The second purpose, interrelated with the first, is to inform various practices by practitioners. Marketers, brand managers, and industry professionals increasingly need to understand and work with fandoms. Understanding the passionate engagement behind fandom makes tremendously good sense from a business perspective. Yet, managers who dive for treasure in the shark-infested seas of brand-fan interactions know that it is a high-risk, high-reward adventure. Our core advice is simple: above all, do no harm. We are not trying to teach you how to exploit fandom. Quite the opposite, we want to teach you how to build a constructive relationship that respects and values the existing relationship between fans and any fan objects you may be working with.

There are also practitioners on the fandom side: the fans themselves and those who assist them. Fandoms are interrelated organizations that are also independent from corporations and individuals who manage the objects of their fandom. Fans and fandoms sue companies, are sued by them, or they sue each other. Similarly, fandoms are financially important, and we believe they are culturally important, too.

We have both been working with organizations in these areas for decades, and our combined experiences have led us to believe that we can provide valuable information to better guide businesses and organizations alike. What is this valuable information? It is practical knowledge. Being useful requires us to blend the academic rigor of fan studies and consumer research with the pragmatic insights of brand management and marketing strategy.

The third purpose of this book is to build on, promote, and try to further the new and important field of fandom relations. In both of our native academic fields—marketing and consumer research, and communication and fan studies—researchers have long recognized that consumers are far from the passive dupes, observers, and recipients that earlier theories and assumptions had made them out to be. Instead, fans, fandoms, consumers, and consumer collectives are enmeshed in complex and passionate relationships with the very brands and franchises that shaped their lives.

We consider the *Frames of Fandom* series to be more than explanatory literature, more than a business guide, and more than a source of inspiration for fan organizations. To match the reality of fandom today, we offer you a series that may shatter categories. We believe *Frames of Fandom* breaks new ground on nearly every page and reflects our insights into bridging our respective fields. It is not a rehash of established wisdom but rather a consolidation of original and, in some cases, controversial thinking.

About this Book and its Authors

Most students cannot name the authors of their textbooks. After all, it is assumed that the textbook's author is an "expert." The faculty teaching the books surely knows the identity of the authors. However, the textbook author's role is to write in a neutral voice, summarizing the indisputable facts of the field rather than sharing the objects of their own passion and curiosity. They are not trying to make an original contribution. Their personalities are masked, and most textbooks bore students to tears. They could have just as easily been written by artificial intelligence (AI). Such lifeless prose seems inappropriate to fans and fandom—topics that are all about passion and personal investments. The field of fandom studies has long focused attention on the positionality of the researcher—that is, our relationship to the objects of our study.

This book is not a textbook in the same vein as that mentioned above. This book grew from two lifetimes of conversations with media, family and friends, other fans, other scholars, and, perhaps most centrally, conversations with each other. As we are about to relate to you, we've recently had the privilege of developing those conversations much further while teaching a course called Fan Relations, which we designed together at the University of Southern California's Annenberg School for Communication and Journalism.

The resulting series of books is an ongoing conversation about the intersection of fan studies and marketing. We have spent many long hours talking about how to bring that conversational quality to the book, and what you are reading is the result. Many multi-authored books hide the individuality of their authors, but it seemed like there was no way to do that with this book, and there was no need to. The two of us have distinct voices, but the conversations we have always had were about bringing our viewpoints together into something new.

You may find one of our voices stronger than another in any given chapter or passage, reflecting where these different conceptual frames come from. However, we both contributed to every text in this series. To continually signal our stakes in this research, we, at times, hold onto the first person to describe our own experiences and insights. Where this happens, look for the phrase "Rob Here" or "Henry here" at the start of a subchapter. To transition to our collective voice, we will often signal with a "both here" designation. In other places, we simply refer to ourselves as "we" and offer our work in the third person. We hope this doesn't become too confusing.

You may also have noticed that this book, like the others in this series, was self-published on Amazon. Although we have a wealth of experience working with academic publishers, we have been less than satisfied with our ability to get our message out in forms that were appropriate to us and our readers. For this reason, we offer these books at a reasonable price and in a slim form that would have likely been impossible for us to arrange with a traditional academic publisher. As a further benefit, we could take control of book marketing and, potentially, more fairly compensate ourselves for our efforts.

Henry and Rob have both fan and professional interests in the topics discussed. One or another of us maintains social relations with most of the other scholars we reference here. They are our mentors, students, colleagues, and friends. We have learned from them, and they have drawn on our research within the network of knowledge production that constitutes any academic field. This is especially the case with fields like fandom studies and consumer culture research, both of which are relatively small by disciplinary standards. Although we will be discussing what we see as some key strands of research within our respective fields, we process them through the lenses of two lifetimes of active research and active participation within fan communities.

And now, we invite you to read and enjoy our exploration of the world of fandom with this second book of the series: **Fandom as Audience**.

CHAPTER 1:

Looking at the Audience

What Makes an Audience Great?

"You are such a great audience." You have probably heard something like this said a thousand times during live performances following the end of a song or before the performer takes their bow, but what does it actually mean? What makes an audience a great audience? In this chapter, we are going to begin our investigation of audiences by lifting the hood on the idea of an audience and kicking the tires on what we know about them.

In its most basic sense, an audience refers to a group of individuals who are listening to or watching the same performance or program, usually at the same time. The origins of the word audience lie in the Latin word *audire*, meaning "to hear." But an audience's hearing of a performance is much more than simply receiving sound waves, which is an automatic physiological process that does not require effort or attention. A quiet audience, a group of people who are sitting still and listening attentively to a live performance, would probably not be called great—at least in most contexts, perhaps at a snooker or golf game where small, polite little claps are the order of the day. Instead, a performer on stage would probably tell an audience that they are great when they are listening *and* responding, probably by applauding enthusiastically, laughing or gasping at the right places, or singing along. The feedback from the audience would indicate not only that they were hearing but also that they were actively listening and even passionately engaged in the unfolding performance. That act of active listening will require not simple physiological reception but focused attention, intention, and a conscious effort to understand, enjoy, imagine, and otherwise participate in the performance.

In the context of live performances, those in attendance are often referred to as "spectators," derived from the Latin word *spectare*, which means to gaze at or observe. The word is related both etymologically and conceptually to "spectacle," which Vincent Kauffman (2006, p. 160), following Guy Debord (whose Situationist work we engage with in **Fandom as Co-creation**) equates with a "subjugation of the world to the economy, the fetishism of goods, reification, alienation, ideology, and specifically, how images, representation, and entertainment prevent authentic life from coming into being." Spectacle is intimately bound up in the idea that consumer culture and mass culture commodify and subvert authentic participation, deflect critical reflection, and pacify by staging larger-than-life events that displace people from the public realm to the marketplace.

However, the types of gatherings we often see around these events defy the passivity and lack of engagement attributed to audiences. Contrary to what some might assume, spectacle is not the type of spectatorship that usually unfolds at sporting events. Certainly, sports spectators observe and watch what is happening at the event. Yet, sports audiences energize their teams by cheering, chanting team anthems, and reacting vocally to the game's highs and lows. This type of audience participation can boost player morale and inspire heightened performance, especially during critical moments of the game. Fans scream and shout, clap and stomp, and may use vuvuzelas, drums, or clappers to increase the noise level. Some sports fans might wave towels or colorful signs to distract opposing teams, creating what they hope will be a home-field advantage. The loud, distracting, and intimidating atmosphere can disrupt opposing teams, affecting their communication, concentration, and perhaps sense of self-assurance. The audience's reactions to player and referee performances—applauding a good play or booing a bad call—can also influence the referees' and players' perceptions and decisions. Their immediate feedback creates a dynamic interaction between the field and the stands. Sports audiences are engaged in a very active form of participation, which itself is an integral part of the live performance.

From Kayfabe and Tifo Banners to Tailgating: Audience Activities

The fandom surrounding WWE wrestling (Ford, 2018; Ford, 2019) is especially interesting in this regard. Scholars such as Benjamin Litherland (2014) have written about the concept of "kayfabe," the awareness audiences have of being inside or outside the fictions around which the events are structured. Originally, there was little acknowledgment that professional wrestling was performed and the outcome was predetermined, so those not in the know were regarded as "rubes" and "marks" (old circus and carnival terms for spectators who were easily fooled in the P.T. Barnum "Never give a sucker an even break" sense).

Today, though, most fans are in on the joke and often stage their enthusiasm for each other. They, in effect, perform as an audience, behaving as though what they see in the ring is real, even though they know it is in some sense "fake," despite the fact the wrestlers really are falling from great heights and smashing tables. Similarly, the crowd may chant "boring" if they are not being entertained (Jenkins, 2013). Because these events are often televised live, such chants signal this disappointment to a broader public and may threaten to disrupt the broadcast. The event promoters respond quickly when this response gets vocalized by trying to speed up a fight that has run its course or to shift the dynamic. Here, the referee functions as the mediator between the booth and the wrestlers in the ring, whispering the next steps to the fighters. Certain performers, such as Hulk Hogan, learned to milk the audience's response, when, seemingly battered and defeated, his arm falling limp, he would rally again, cheered on by the fans. Pumped up, he turns the match around, and we see an almost literal version of the idea that an enthusiastic audience energizes the performer.

Sports spectators also bring banners and signs to the game to visually demonstrate their allegiance and support. Large, coordinated displays, like card stunts or tifo displays in soccer (a tifo is a visual display of flags, signs, or banners made by fans in a soccer stadium), add to the spectacle and express collective support. Sports games are spectacles in which many spectators wear their team colors on jerseys, uniforms, caps, hats, and other clothes or through other visual signals of affiliation. The large screens in big stadiums often feature the most elaborately dressed or decorated fans. At a Los Angeles Chargers game Rob attended in November 2024 at SoFi Stadium, he noted the range of sports costumes that blended superhero and sports motifs to express a type of syncretic super-fandom. He saw one fan wearing an Iron Man mask on top of his all-body LA Chargers uniform. The mask was in the team's metallic powder blue and gold colors, which worked well as a variation of the Iron Man colors. Another fan was wearing an LA Chargers-colored Boba Fett mask over his uniform.

Many sports fans engage in pre-game, in-game, and post-game rituals that enhance the communal experience, providing experiences of fandom that extend their presence as spectators or audience members. This might include performing specific cheers at certain game points, singing particular songs at predetermined times, or tailgating Today, tailgating is commonly understood in America as a social gathering that often includes grilling, eating, drinking, and socializing in advance of some events, such as a sporting event. The research of Tonya Williams Bradford and John Sherry, which we also explore in **Fandom as Consumer Collective**, considers the nature of tailgating as a cultural practice that is deeply embedded both in American history and in contemporary sports culture. They conducted a detailed ethnographic study of collegiate football practices in the Midwestern United States that explains how tailgating blends domestic rituals with public celebration, reflects cultural traditions, but also serves as a site of civic and social engagement centered around sports (Bradford and Sherry, 2015). Linking the public practice of tailgating to the ancient Greek symposium and Roman convivium (p. 134), they are considered forebears of modern tailgaters. These spectators arrived with picnic baskets full of food and wine to watch the Battle of Bull Run in 1861 during the American Civil War. This tradition of combining food and socializing with public spectacles extended to other notable events, such as atomic bomb tests in the 1950s, where civilians gathered to observe the tests in a similarly communal manner.

Bradford and Sherry trace the roots of sports-related tailgating to the first intercollegiate football game between Princeton and Rutgers in 1869. This historic match established a precedent for linking sports events with public gatherings, food, and festivity (ibid). Over time, tailgating evolved alongside the growth of football culture, cementing its place as an integral part of game-day traditions. By the mid-20th century, it had become a widespread ritual at collegiate and professional football games, drawing elements of domesticity, celebration, and fandom together and combining them with drinking and feasting.

An estimated 70 million people participate annually in tailgate parties in the United States (Bradford and Sherry, 2015). The evolution of tailgate parties reflects broader societal changes, including the increasing role of fan community gatherings in shaping a sense of popular cultural identity. While tailgating has expanded to other events, such as concerts, its strongest association remains with American football, where it continues to thrive as a cornerstone of game-day rituals.

The Book's Cover Image

The photograph on this book's cover offers another glimpse into what an ideal audience might look like in a different cultural context. In this case, the shot (taken by Henry) depicts the full house at a concert given in Ningbo, China, by Taiwanese pop star A-Lin in the Summer of 2024. Though frequently associated with K-pop, light sticks are ubiquitous throughout East Asian idol culture. In this case, they are simple and generic (and buckled to the seats to avoid being stolen). Anyone who bought a ticket has access to them and utilizes them as an expression of their enthusiasm for the performance. Good audiencing requires the collective deployment of light sticks at certain moments. The light sticks flash or turn colors according to central programming so that the audience becomes part of the collective performance. If one could look at the intensity of the expressions on the audience members' faces as they wave the light sticks, one thing becomes clear: they want to get this right; they want to signal their support. We might think of these sticks as having the same purpose as cigarette lighters among rock fans or now the flashlight function on people's smartphones.

Hardcore fans may acquire and possess their own, more elaborate versions of these light sticks so that they may be displayed as a sign of their fandom outside the performance arena. Henry sought a lightstick to show his support for his favorite K-pop group, (G)I-dle during a trip to Seoul, but could not find them in any of the K-pop shops he visited. During his trip to Ningbo, China, he met a fellow fan who helped him acquire one through her connections to a fan network. In Figure 1.1, we see the two of them celebrating their purchase together. The purple glow and the Wonderland Castle inside, even the bulb's shape, are details recognized by other fans as part of the semiotics of (G)I-dle's lightstick (Henry is also wearing a t-shirt connected with the group as he learns how to be a better K-pop fan).

Figure 1.1: Henry and a fellow [G]I-dle fan celebrating the lightstick acquisition in Ningbo, Korea (photo © Henry Jenkins)

How We Learned to Audience

Our contemporary understanding of what constitutes a great audience is the byproduct of more than a hundred years of concentrated efforts by theater owners and elite critics to police and train working class audiences so that they would behave according to middle class expectations. John E. Kasson's *Rudeness and Civility* (1990) offers perhaps the best account of this process. His discussion of "The Disciplining of Spectatorship" comes at the end of a book that explored shifts in table manners, emotional expression, and public behavior in 19th-century urban United States. This policing of private conduct would result in the expectation that those forms of entertainment soliciting middle class and female patronage would require similar conduct in public settings. As Kasson writes, "the expressive, often rowdy, male-dominated assemblies that played so conspicuous a part in the first part of the century were increasingly challenged by disciplined, passive and segmented gatherings in which middle-class women figured prominently" (p. 215).

We might compare the depiction of the aggressive reception that greets a Shakespearean performance in John Ford's classic western, *My Darling Clementine* with the depiction of early 20th-century opera audiences in the second season of *The Gilded Age* to understand the shifts Kason was describing. Both are more or less historically accurate for the time they are set. In between the two was an incident known as the Astor Place Riots,

Audiencing, observing, and spectating are all related notions. Each suggests some level of dispassion or distance in relating the performance on stage to those who sit in the seats, stand, or otherwise witness it. Note our somewhat awkward but intentional use of "audiencing" as a verb here. For us, people are not simply part of an audience; audiencing is something that a person does—a set of shared activities and stances that have various manifestations. As you may have already begun to appreciate, the notion of acting as an audience is often much more complex than these neutralizing, disinterested, and straightforward terms would suggest.

Audience Psychology

There is a long history of speculation and research on the psychology of the audience. Work in this area goes back to Coleman R. Griffith's (1921, p. 36) examination of students attending a live lecture in an "all-to-one" format. Interestingly, Coleman found that where students sat in relation to the speaker did not affect their grades;

however, what did affect them was how socially integrated that audience member was among the group. This emphasis on group integration is an intriguing way to begin a field of audience study because it points not to internal individual characteristics but to the relationships of individuals in a collective. In a way, this finding drives us toward the notion of the audience member as a participant in a social group: a type of fandom.

Much more recently, social psychologists, including many in marketing-related fields, have been fascinated by how imagination is involved in the individual reception of stories. In a conceptual meta-analysis, consumer researcher and narrative specialist Tom van Laer and his colleagues (van Laer et al., 2014) examined how different types of stories— from books and music lyrics to advertising, retail, and travel—are consumed by consumers and, in the process, become what the authors call "narratives." They also found that the receivers of stories have considerable amounts of agency in how they interpret stories.

a public misconduct that erupted in response to a feud between two great actors of the late 19th century, Edwin Forrest and William Charles McReady. Forrest's enthusiasts were predominantly working class, whereas McReady appealed to the growing American middle class. When Forrest supporters booed and heckled McReady as pompous and prissy, fisticuffs broke out, and a stampede out of the theater killed 22 people and sent more than a hundred to local hospitals. As Kason describes the event, "thousands of working men outside bombarded the theater with paving stones and tried to storm the entrance—whereupon the militia fired upon them" (p. 228).

The shock of this incident increased already simmering middle class anxiety about sharing the theater with these ruffians. Prices were raised, segmented seating was implemented, and an effort was made to instruct patrons how to behave appropriately. Such issues continued into the early history of the cinema, where women were frightened to sit in the dark next to strange men who could be mashers, and slides projected onto the screen asked women to remove their hats, attendees not to vocalize their responses to the movies, or men to limit smoking and other potentially disturbing behavior. These regulatory moves were part of the deliberate transformation of movies from a predominantly working class and immigrant-based form of popular entertainment (as they were in the early days) into a form safe for middle class patrons who would become the primary audience from the early 1910s onward. A similar effort to instruct behavior continues today: the Alamo Drafthouse theater chain, for example, refuses to seat patrons after the film has begun, has a notice to turn off your cell phone, and has a system for spectators to communicate with the staff if someone near them is being disruptive.

These efforts to reform the spectator's spontaneous reactions play a central role in the early history of United States fandom, with the passionate engagement of fans often perceived as increasing the dangers of rowdy and disruptive mob behavior (Cavicchi, 2018). The term "fan" would have been anachronistic at the time of the Astor Place riots. Still, the description of the war between "enthusiasts" for different actors who had conflicting ideas about who they wanted to attract to their performances parallel some of the contemporary fan wars between pop divas and their fans.

To understand how historical narratives are commercialized and consumed, Athinodoros Chronis (2008) conducted in-depth interviews with tourists visiting the American Civil War Museum and taking the Gettysburg Tour in Gettysburg, Virginia. He discovered there were numerous ways these visitors consumed Gettysburg's historical stories in the museum and while on tour, several of which might be viewed as resistant or oppositional. When a tourist guide explained something about Gettysburg's history, the tourists themselves voiced their prior knowledge, which sometimes led them to contest the version conveyed by the designated storyteller. They could also fill in gaps in the stories they found in the museum and on the tour. They recontextualized the Gettysburg story by comparing it to events in their own personal experiences. They would also extend the historical narrative by engaging imaginatively with it.

This imaginative engagement is crucial to the consumption of stories. When consumers read stories, they may engage in "narrative transportation," psychologist Richard Gerrig's (1993) term for being so engrossed in a story that the story's receiver feels carried away by it, in a process that involves both empathy and mental imagery. These processes can have major impacts on emotions, intentions, persuasion, and behaviors. The key point is that when psychologists consider a single audience member receiving a story, whether in a movie theater, a concert hall, or at a political rally, they find a wealth of activity in their imagination and a number of effects. Although it might appear they are just sitting there, blank, passive, and mostly immobile spectators, the real activity is happening in the mysterious space between their ears.

Finally, we can consider another internal process that directly relates to audiences and imagination. In an age where audience members can easily become content creators, research into how these culture producers think about their audiences is increasingly salient. A range of studies have examined how different content producers have imagined the audience for their content. These studies build upon Benedict Anderson's (1985) notion of the "imagined community," which is formed by print media and is held to underlie nationalism in the modern nation-state. The concept of the "imagined audience" is the mental construct that a content producer has about who is receiving their content. Influenced by a range of factors, the content producer's concept of the imagined audience seems significant in digital environments like social media, where actual audiences are large, diverse, and often invisible, making it challenging for content creators to know exactly who they might be communicating with. We will return to this question of the imagined audience in our discussion of transmedia storytelling and its consumption.

Eden Litt's (2012) article "Knock, Knock. Who's There? The Imagined Audience," for example, peers into the complexities of how individuals conceptualize their audiences in digital communication spaces, particularly in social media. Mark Coddington, Seth Lewis, and Valerie Belair-Gagnon (2021) research how journalists conceptualize their audience and the sources of these perceptions. The study utilizes a survey of American journalists to uncover that these perceptions come from a mix of personal, social, and institutional interactions, including email, social media, and professional relationships.

Writers and producers often form mental images of their fan audience, envisioning them as the receivers of their work. These imaginary concepts might be close to reality, or they may bear very little resemblance to actual audiences. We find the concept of imaginary fan communities intriguing and important, and we hope these ideas will inspire future scholarship in the field.

Viewing Audiences

People are usually interested in audiences for a specific reason and view them from a particular perspective. Media, technology, and advertising companies all make money based on measurements of the size and engagement levels of their audiences, just as influencers do. In that sense, entrepreneurs are interested in audiences. Even politicians are concerned with audiences; some of them are even obsessed with the size of the live crowds they can draw.

The idea of an audience, the measurement of the size and activity of an audience, and the qualities of an audience are crucial for both academic research and industry practice. And yet, with the proliferation of media channels and rapid changes in technologies, the concept of the audience is increasingly complex. Rob Eagle, Rik Lander, and Phil Hall (2021) studied the audience of a live performance of a generative AI show called *I am Echoborg* and found that their responses to the show were nuanced and strategic. Neither wholly positive nor negative, audience responses involved learning about the system and communicating with other audience members. Increasingly, situations arise in which AI performs for various types of audiences, sometimes with their awareness and at other times when the audience is unsuspecting.

Communication scholar Jim Webster (1998) usefully reviews the various theoretical frameworks used to study media (but not live performance) audiences, including the effects model, uses and gratifications, and reception studies. Calling for a more interdisciplinary approach that acknowledges the multifaceted nature of media audience behavior, Jim develops a framework that organizes audience studies perspectives into three basic yet intersecting models: "*audience-as-mass, audience-as-outcome*, and *audience-as-agent*" (p. 191). We have adapted Webster's article's helpful ideas and diagram into what we call "a syncretic view of the audience," which we model in Figure 1.2.

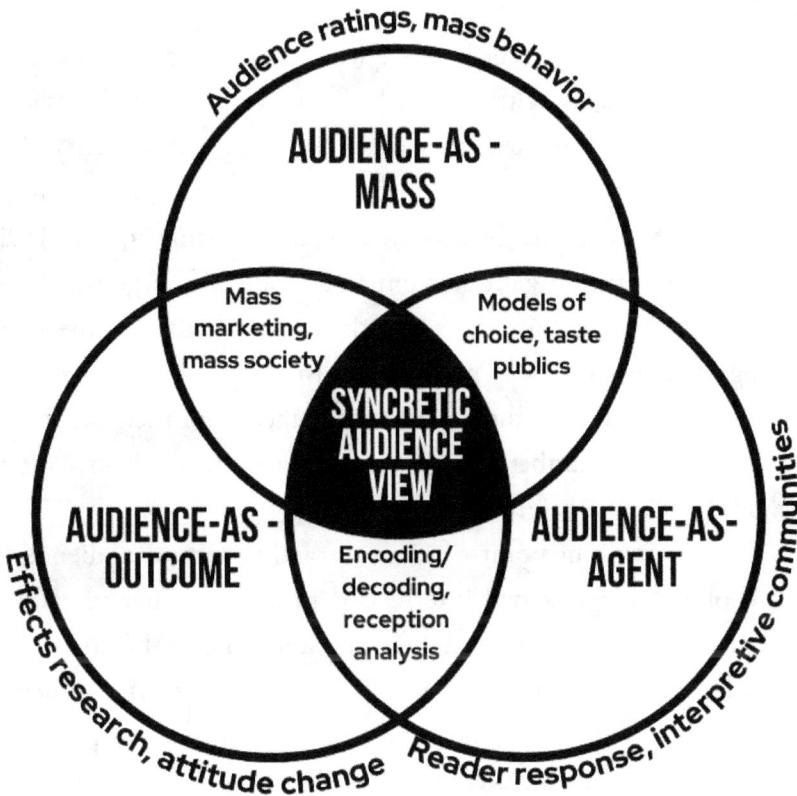

Figure 1.2: A Syncretic View of the Audience, adapted from Webster (1998) (source: author created image)

Audience-as-Mass

The first perspective, "audience as mass," views the audience as a large, undifferentiated group that passively receives content and messages from mass media channels such as radio, television, and newspapers. This perspective is rooted in the Industrial Revolution and the rise of mass media; it focuses on the quantitative measurement of audience behavior, primarily through methods like surveys and Nielsen audience ratings. These methods aggregate data and then statistically manipulate it, aiming to predict general media consumption patterns and preferences by viewing them as mass behavior.

Consider major television events such as the FIFA World Cup, Olympic Games, or Super Bowl. With events such as these, broadcasters and advertisers try to reach a massive group with a single message to maximize their reach and advertising impact. They view the audience not as a collection of different groups but as a single population unto itself. Obviously, this massification ignores individual differences to gain economies of scale and large numbers. Even more dramatic are the network economies driving the marketing strategies of social media platforms such as Instagram and WeChat. The value of these platforms comes from their capability to attract large numbers of users and aggregate them in various ways for mass campaigns.

From a fandom point of view, attracting a mass audience to a fan object suggests two interrelated principles. First, the sheer size of the audience means there is probably a normal distribution of audience engagement at work. Most members of the audience are only mildly engaged, and others, a much smaller percentage, are passionately engaged. However, with large numbers, this likely means that a significant amount of fans are passionately engaged with the fan object. This leads to the second insight: the mass effects model does not reveal who these passionately engaged audience members are. With this model, they are hidden in the mass. To understand who these engaged audience members are or to connect with and assist them, mass measurement methods such as overall ratings based on surveys or online reach and subscriber numbers will not help.

The perspective that favors mass ratings over more subtle differentiation of audience engagement has sometimes been called valuing impressions over expressions. Cristel Russell et al. (2004) developed and tested a useful "connectedness scale" to help distinguish audience members who have intense relationships with television programs and their charac-ters. As they explain it:

> One of the main contributions of the connectedness scale is overcoming the limited nature of previous audience measures based on audience size or volume of viewing, attitude towards the program, or even involvement. As a more descriptive and qualitatively rich measure of audiences, connectedness provides new directions for this area of research (p. 160).

Although the audience-as-mass model is useful for some purposes and in certain situations, measures such as connectedness and engagement provide methods that are more attuned to the passionate pursuits of fans and members of fandoms. More nuanced, distinctive, and emotion-driven ways to understand audiences and their different actors, like Russell et al.'s (2004) connectedness scale, can be applied to not only understand television audiences but also to measure connection with sports and sports figures, music and music artists, and other forms of entertainment, too. Measures such as these serve as a useful extension to massified audience segmentation strategies.

Audience-as-Outcome

The "audience-as-outcome" perspective emphasizes the effects media have on audiences, focusing on how content and the characteristics of different media influence audience behavior and attitudes. This approach is based on Shannon and Weaver's (1948) transmission model of communication, which asserts that media messages are transmitted by a sender (media producer) and subsequently received by an audience, potentially leading to measurable effects on their knowledge, attitudes, or behaviors. In a later chapter, we will discuss the encoding/decoding framework, which is Stuart Hall's useful cultural extension of this basic formulation.

Outcomes are important. Sports broadcasters want to attract big audiences so that they can sell advertising. Advertisers want to reach large audiences so that members will buy their products and services. Musicians get more money when a greater number of people stream their music, attend their concerts, and purchase their merchandise. All of these actions are media effects. The reason someone conceptualizes the audience as an outcome is because they want to understand how to create these types of effects (see our discussion of "activation" below). Media is financed because of its capacity not only to inform but also to persuade: to change attitudes, shape public opinion, and influence cultural norms. In fandom studies, audience researchers seek to understand the types of effects resulting from participating in fandom, whether these are commercial effects such as collecting, identity effects such as displaying fandom on a t-shirt, organizing effects such as starting a fan collective, or creative effects such as contributing fan fiction or art.

Consider the role of television campaigns in public health—such as anti-smoking ads or promoting COVID-19 vaccination—which demonstrate how media can be strategically used to affect audience health behaviors on a large scale. In the digital age, the "audience-as-outcome" model also informs the strategies behind social media campaigns and word-of-mouth or viral marketing. Platforms such as YouTube and TikTok leverage reach and personalized content to influence viewer behaviors. Whether seeking to increase the intention to purchase a brand of toothpaste or spur social action on reproductive rights, the measurable outcomes of such campaigns demonstrate that this audience concept enjoys continued relevance.

The Audience-as-Agents View

Conceptualizing the audience as dynamic participants who selectively engage with media based on their personal needs, interests, and socio-cultural contexts is Webster's third conceptualization. This perspective is most closely aligned with the fandom studies and participatory culture perspective because it acknowledges the agency of audience members in choosing and interpreting media content in ways that matter to them and mirror their own experiences (see the sidebar, "Henry on Agency and Autonomy").

An audience-as-agents model is clearly visible in the realm of social media, where Web 2.0 types of affordances enable a wide variety of media content users to also become interactive creators and curators. For instance, listeners can choose podcasts that cater to niche interests or specific professional fields. The members of contemporary online audiences are not limited to some editor's choices in a daily newspaper; instead, they are often busily pursuing different media paths, such as tailoring their social media subscriptions and feeds to match the specific interests and viewpoints that interest them in the present. The ability to subscribe, download, watch, and listen to a massive array of diverse content at any time further underscores the plenitudinous and choice-driven state of contemporary audiences. Consider how few of the posts shared with you every day you read and how few of these you choose to recirculate or discuss with others in your network. This is very different from the massified wholes of the audience-as-mass view of Nielsen ratings. The agentic audience is composed of people who are united in determining their own unique media experiences.

Evidence of the agentic nature of fan audiences is all around us. Taylor Swift's concerts in Vienna were originally scheduled for August 8th, 9th, and 10th, 2024 but had to be canceled due to a foiled plot by Islamic State terrorists. The cancellation left tens of thousands of fans, including Rob's Austrian cousins (who had been planning their outfits and other elements of the event for months), devastated. However, Rob was heartened to get Instagram posts on the days that the concert was supposed to be held. Gathering in the streets of Vienna, this almost-audience actively transformed their collective disappointment into celebration. One of the main meeting points was the Corneliusgasse because Swift has a song named "Cornelia Street." They also met at Stephansplatz, in the center of Vienna. They wore their outfits, held up their signs, sang Taylor Swift songs, swayed under their upheld lit cellphones, and shared stories about their fanship of the global superstar. One of their main activities was to gather to trade friendship bracelets, a tradition observed by fans at Eras Tour shows, and hang them on trees. We have more to say about these bracelets in **Fandom as Participatory Culture.**

Through these activities, although the original concert performance had been canceled, these fans still gathered, forming an audience in which they participated by performing for each other in various ways. The image in Figure 1.3 is a screenshot from a smartphone video shot by Rob's Viennese cousin, who was at the event. The video features a large gathering of people singing the lyrics to Taylor Swift's "Blank Space" and applauding themselves afterward.

Figure 1.3: Viennese Street-gathering in Lieu of the Cancelled Taylor Swift Concert (photo courtesy of Marlene Weischelbaum).

HENRY ON AGENCY AND AUTONOMY

For me, agency has to do with issues of self-representation and self-determination within the contested spaces that shape our everyday lives. Agency, in that sense, is both personal (how much control do I have over how I perceive and act upon the world?) and collective (how much power do I gain by joining forces with others to pursue shared interests?).

Agency is not the same thing as autonomy. We make choices in a world not of our own making and not of our own choosing. There are constraints or limits on what we can do, what we can see, and what we can think, but for that very reason, it is important to recognize the freedom to think and act, which we do enjoy within those constraints.

Agency is closely related to notions of voice, which Nick Couldry (2010) has defined as the capacity to construct and circulate representations of oneself that matter, that can make sense to others, and that may have consequences in terms of how they perceive you and what actions they take that impact your life. Giving voice to our concerns is one way that people exercise agency.

In cultural studies, agency often exists in relation to structure: none of us, as I suggested above, have absolute autonomy. Our agency is constrained or reshaped by various systemic and structural factors in our lives. Our ability to act in the world is shaped by our access to knowledge, to a shared vocabulary

Viewing audiences as participants emphasize media consumption as an interactive, on-demand, and personalized process. It views the audience not as a homogeneous mass but as a collection of agentic individuals whose interactions with media are shaped by a complex interplay of personal preferences, social influences, and cultural contexts. Yet it may be worthwhile to consider whether being an agentic audience member is necessarily the same thing as being an active one.

Structuring Audiences

In a pertinent provocation, Webster (1998) suggests that audience studies should "abandon" the terms "active" and "passive" as defining polarities of the field because they focus too much on micro-level interactions, undervalue the role of habit, and focus insufficient attention on the audience as a mass phenomenon (p. 202). Instead, citing the prominent sociologist Anthony Giddens (1987, pp. 220–21), he recommends considering audiences in terms of agency and structure.

Structure is the very medium of the 'human' element of human agency. At the same time, agency is the medium of structure, which individuals routinely reproduce in the course of their activities... Human beings normally know not only what they are doing at any moment, but why they are doing it. That is to say, it is characteristic of human agents that they routinely appraise what they do as a means of doing it, and that they are able discursively to give both an account of what they do and of their reasons for what they do... But it does not follow that they know all there is to know about the consequences of what they do, for the activities of others or for their own activities in the future. Nor do they know all there is to know all about the conditions of their action, that is, the circumstances that are causally involved with its production.

through which to express our experiences, to the platforms through which we speak, to the willingness of others to listen and take seriously what it is we are trying to communicate, and so forth. Agency is impacted by structural and systemic inequalities around issues of age and generation, race and ethnicity, gender and sexuality, and class and economic opportunity.

–From Interview with Neil Anderson (2017)

Webster argues that, like viewing audiences through a syncretic lens, the structure-agency approach to understanding audiences effectively merges the traditional active/passive audience dichotomy within a broader framework of agency. It acknowledges that while individuals are generally self-aware, they may not fully grasp the implications or origins of their actions. The concept of structure, encompassing elements like group memberships, professions, social classes, media markets, or technological infrastructures, is likely to be an important part of our explanations about how fans engage with their fan objects and how these interactions shape collective behaviors.

Fans are agentic when they actively select and interpret media content. Yet, their choices are shaped by available media, their own social, racial, class, and other personal situations, societal norms, and the infrastructural and economic conditions of the media landscape. These conditions facilitate or constrain their fan activities, highlighting the reciprocal relationship between fans agency and the panoply of structural forces at play. For example, in **Defining Fandom**, both Rob and Henry describe becoming fans of television shows that were available to them. *Batman, Star Trek,* and *Gilligan's Island* were all syndicated programs that were broadcast often and at times when the authors could watch them. Although both authors played participatory roles in their use of these media, they had to first gain access to them. While popular and widely viewed in reruns, *Gilligan's Island* did not gather a significant fandom around it, while the other two series did. This is another structural difference, one that illustrates the indeterminacy of fan agency. Both authors were also exposed to some of their fanships by their families.

Although we appreciate Webster's points about looking at the contexts in which fan audiences develop and thrive, we would not want to abandon the notion of audience activity or downplay its importance. By closely attending to and theorizing various types of audience activity—in particular, the varied, collective, and creative kinds of activity we are talking about concerning fanships and fandom—we learn a great deal about what these fans actually do. Much of this book is concerned with providing details about the hidden ways audiences engage with media and other fan objects. We do not see a need to choose either active/passive or structure/agency distinctions. We like both/and choices rather than either/or. We can keep them both in mind and see analytic occasions where one might be more useful than the other.

Focusing exclusively on structure and agency implies that ostensibly causal explanations are preferable to richly descriptive and interpretative understandings, and we reject this popular positivist assumption as wrong-headed. Having a more refined focus on both activity and agency enhances the foundational models of audience, providing an opportunity for explanatory and descriptive insights into traditional questions about media interaction. What would appear to be critical to our understanding is not simply avoiding the activity/passive polarity that Webster argues is a defining element of audience studies. Instead, what is needed is to avoid the assumption of passivity that seems baked into the etymology and definition of terms like audience and spectator, and to vigilantly avoid acting as if these assumptions were actually true.

De-individuating the Audience

It seems clear that the definition of "audience" has evolved over time. Previously, an audience was typically defined as a group of people who were physically present in the same place and at the same time to witness some event, such as a theatrical performance or a sports event. However, as mass communication has taken over the way people consume entertainment and related events, the meaning of "audience" has expanded to include groups that engage with the same content, even if they do so remotely or asynchronously through television, radio, or the internet. Therefore, we can now speak of a single "audience" for a viral YouTube video, even though that audience might comprise people who live in dozens of different countries and watch the video over the span of months or years.

Webster (1998, p. 200) cautions audience researchers not to reduce mass communication, such as we would find in studies of fans and fandoms, "to a matter of individual responses" observed through ethnography or with experimental subjects, lone readers or individuals operating within the bounds of family or group membership. "Most empirical research into mass media communicators' audience images has been microscopic—more productive of closeups than panoramas" (Blumler, 1996, p. 99). The contemporary emphasis on digital engagement—likes, reposts, and comments—recapitulates this microscopic focus by homing in on individual responses and then aggregating them.

Social collectives are more than simple aggregations of individuals. Webster affirms that prior research reveals that audiences have characteristics that are invisible at lower levels of analysis and that we can learn a lot "by considering the audience as a social force in its own right" (p. 201). On digital platforms, this may mean taking a socially embedded view of the audience as an ongoing conversation between many different social actors connected at different times and in many ways.

As **Defining Fandoms** explores, being a member of a fandom means an entirely new set of relationships that alters and exponentially extends the audience affiliation by bridging it with a set of social connections. Unpacking specific differences—in people's characteristics, in audience situations, in temporal and cultural contexts, for example—is going to be key to building lasting and sophisticated understandings of fans, fandoms, and audiences. Consider that live sporting events, conventions, and concerts are highlights, if not core events, in some fans' lives. Audience models such as Webster's may miss much about fandom when they exclude these powerful, passion-building, and enthusiasm-expressing events. Furthermore, Webster's model was created for a mass media age that no longer exists in the same form; the way we interact with digital media has altered not just the nature of being an audience member but also the nature of membership in fandom.

Thinking About Audiences

As we conclude this chapter, we can observe that the evolution from early audience studies to more sophisticated contemporary understandings of fan participation reveals how deeply embedded audience behaviors are within the historical, cultural, and social contexts that give rise to them. From early theatrical performances to modern cinema, spectators were disciplined into appropriate behaviors by physical space but also, increasingly, by regulative norms and structured expectations about how they should interact with it and with each other. As social class distinctions and middle-class values influenced audience behavior, we saw the emergence of a tamer and more obedient spectator as a type of managed ideal, perhaps even an organizational aspiration. Yet, as the field of audience studies evolved, research began to uncover the passionate, energetic, imaginative, and often resistant ways audiences actually engage with media texts. From Coleman Griffith's (1921) early 20th-century research on group dynamics in live settings to more recent studies on narrative transportation, the emphasis shifted from studies of a more receptive spectatorship to ones that recognize the extent to which passionate audiences—let's call them a "great audience"—co-create significance.

This progression in audience studies naturally leads to a focus on how fans, as passionate and especially engaged audience members, are participants who play a range of roles that shape the meaning, reception, and commercial success of media products. As we transition into our book's next chapter, we shift our attention to how media industries increasingly view audiences as segmented markets and fans as a certain kind of segment within those markets. The rise of digital platforms—accompanied by social media marketing, social media monitoring, and social analytics—has transformed how fans are targeted, categorized, and monetized, with companies developing various strategies to harness fan engagement and loyalty. To fully appreciate the trajectory of audience studies, our investigation would be incomplete without a deeper look into the growing importance of segmentation and targeting in understanding fan audiences as markets and how these processes are applied to monetize fan practices and behaviors in a globalized media landscape.

CHAPTER 2:

Fan Audiences as Markets

The concept of the "target audience" plays a central role in the development of both media industries and marketing strategies. Emerging from the early 20th-century mass media landscape, the target audience concept was fundamentally structured by the needs of advertisers and governments seeking to communicate with specific groups. This marked a significant shift from the mass audience model, which presumed a homogeneous collective, to one where distinct groups could be identified and addressed with specially customized messages. As media diversified, so did audiences. In some sense, the one created the other. The differentiation of media not only responded to differences in audience viewpoints but also amplified and created them (Shrum, 2017). All of this differentiation was driven by the needs of business and government, as a deregulated and privatized media system allowed businesses to follow governments and eventually get much better at precisely targeting audiences through a variety of communication media. The use of psychographics, demographics, and behavioral data to segment markets laid the foundation for how we approach audiences today.

Fan audiences as markets are shaped by both precise targeting and unexpected fan-driven success. Netflix's *Wednesday* succeeded by aggregating multiple fan bases, while *The Hunger Games'* Capitol Collection failed by misunderstanding its core audience. Motion pictures like *Fantasia* and *The Rocky Horror Picture Show*, which initially missed their mark, later became cult classics through unanticipated fan engagement. On the other hand, the *Spider-Man* franchises have consistently targeted younger demographics with crossover potential. These examples show that while segmentation and targeting are essential, fan response often adds unpredictable value, turning niche properties into broad successes.

However, the application of these traditional marketing strategies to fan audiences is still, we hesitate to say, a bit ham-fisted. We can see that in the awkward marketing that CoverGirl undertook with *The Hunger Games: Catching Fire* or the way Hollywood still depends on clunky "quartiles" to conceptualize customers for its cinematic products. These are cases that we will cover in the following chapters.

For fan audiences, their identities, values, and emotional connections to their fan objects often influence their engagement more than coarse demographic or geographic cues might indicate. Similarly, sociohistorical and cultural contexts, which are constantly changing, matter. That leads to unexpected and unpredictable marketing successes, like those we will discuss relating to Disney and cult movies. Market segmentation, in those cases, becomes less about grouping demographically similar consumers and more about being able to respond by leaning into the participation and creativity that fan cultures bring to the table. This calls for a strategic recalibration, where marketers must not only identify target audiences but also recognize the cultural, social, and emotional factors that drive their fandom.

The transition from mass marketing to fan marketing introduces significant and, we believe, exciting challenges and opportunities. Fandom marketing is a moving target, one we will consider numerous times in numerous ways throughout this book series. One intriguing strategy involves the aggregation of multiple fanships into a viable and pre-approving, as opposed to pre-approved, audience. We use Netflix's *Wednesday* successful multiple fan base aggregation strategy as an example of this practice.

As this chapter unfolds, we will explore how media producers and brands have been drawn to increasingly acknowledge fan audiences as distinct markets within the overall marketplace and to plan accordingly. However, fully realizing this acknowledgment in practice has been elusive. Fan marketing has barely moved beyond the basics of rudimentary demographic profiling and into the complexities of fandoms' collective identities, behaviors, and participatory cultures.

The Target Audience

It is difficult to pinpoint the very first use of the term "target audience." Its origins lie in the early to mid-20th century and are linked to the rise of contemporary mass media like radio and television and their advertising. During this time marked by militarism and business interests, governments and businesses increasingly sought to tailor their messages to specific groups of people. Government documents from the 1940s related to wartime propaganda and public information campaigns were already making use of the term "target audience," suggesting that this utilization predated later business uses. Military involvement in the deployment of more nuanced mass communications accords well with the early history of marketing as an outcropping of military *strategy* and *tactics*—words that are still widely used in marketing and business to the present day.

By the 1950s, the term "target audience" had become established in the marketing and advertising fields. Textbooks and trade publications from this era routinely use the term when discussing how to craft effective advertising campaigns to reach the different types of audiences that gathered for different television and radio shows and in different magazines and newspapers. The usage clearly reflects the growing recognition of the importance of market segmentation and tailored messaging in marketing communication. By the 1960s, the notion of and the phrase "target audience" was even more prevalent, particularly with the rise of television programming and its ostensible separation of audiences into different viewer demographics: children's programming, women's programming, family programming, etc.

Segmenting and Targeting Fan Audiences

In marketing, the idea of targeting is interconnected with the strategy of segmentation. An early and influential piece of marketing scholarship by Wendell Smith (1956, p. 6), written around the time of the rise of the term "target audience," explains the concept of market segmentation as follows:

> viewing a heterogeneous market (one characterized by divergent demand) as a number of smaller homogeneous markets in response to differing product preferences among important market segments. It is attributable to the desires of consumers or users for more precise satisfaction of their varying wants. Like differentiation, segmentation often involves the substantial use of advertising and promotion. This is to inform market segments of the availability of goods or services produced for or presented as meeting their needs with precision... Market

segmentation is essentially a merchandising strategy, merchandising being used here in its technical sense as representing the adjustment of market offerings to consumer or user requirements.

Therefore, as Smith explains it, segmentation becomes the process of taking a multifaceted mass market and dividing it into smaller subgroups that are more similar within themselves than they are between one another (Sarin, 2010). The members assigned to these "homogeneous" subgroups will display similarities in needs, preferences, and/or behaviors. For example, one could segment everyone who uses toothpaste into those who brush their teeth more than three times per day or who only use a particular brand of toothpaste. One could also segment by a particular need, such as having a stronger need for tooth whitening versus breath freshening.

There are four types of characteristics used in segmentation. The first is personal demographics, which include attributes such as age, gender, income, education, occupation, and religion. The second is geographic, which includes general (national, regional) and specific information (neighborhood and postal or zip code) on location. Third is psychographics, which includes elements such as lifestyle variables, personality or psychological characteristics, values, interests, and opinions. Fourth are behavioral characteristics. Before the digital age, behavioral characteristics focused on matters such as usage frequency, length of usage, usage type, specific brand used, and level of brand loyalty.

Today, behavioral targeting leverages user interaction data from various digital and physical touchpoints to create a variety of personalized marketing strategies. By analyzing search terms, page visits, purchase history, session durations, clicks, IP addresses, geolocation, and user login details, marketers can segment into very small audiences—even audiences of one—and deliver tailored content, advertisements, and offers to them. As data analytics and AI have become more powerful and widely available, digital behavioral targeting approaches have become quite sophisticated, with predictive models that promise to (but never completely can) anticipate consumer needs and preferences. Recent developments focus on real-time behavioral tracking, allowing for dynamic personalization during live interactions, such as in-app suggestions, geotargeted offers, or constant retargeting (i.e., those product ads that seem to follow you around wherever you search). In Figure 2.1, we present and explain these four types of segmentation, illustrating how they might be used in fan marketing situations.

DEMOGRAPHICS

- Demographics (age, gender, income, education, occupation) provide insights into population characteristics.
- Help organizations tailor products, services, and marketing strategies to specific groups.
- Example: Knowing audience age helps a music label sign relevant talent or craft album messaging.

PSYCHOGRAPHICS

- Psychographics include values, attitudes, interests, and lifestyles.
- Explore deeper motivations behind choices and worldviews.
- Example: A television producer targeting climate-conscious viewers for a new series with a sustainability based plot.
- Provide a nuanced view beyond demographics for richer consumer insights.

GEOGRAPHY

- Geographic segmentation targets markets based on location.
- Useful for tailoring strategies to local preferences and needs.
- Example: A sports promoter adjusts offerings based on regional weather conditions.

BEHAVIORAL

- Behavioral segmentation categorizes consumers by behaviors like search patterns, purchasing habits, spending patterns, brand loyalty, and usage rates.
- Modern behavioral targeting uses data from digital and physical interactions (e.g., search terms, page visits, purchase history, session duration, clicks, geolocation) for precise personalization.
- Example: Loyal theme park visitors can be targeted with rewards programs, exclusive offers, and personalized recommendations to maintain their engagement.

Figure 2.1: Segmentation in Fan Marketing (source: author created image)

Because organizations, whether governmental or industrial, have limited resources, they cannot reach every segment in a marketplace; therefore, they must concentrate their efforts only on a certain selected segment or segments, which are called (in another application of strategic military language) the target segment. The reason marketers (or pollsters, for that matter) split populations into groups, such as young working women who are anime fans, is not because those groups are interesting to them per se or because of their demographics, interests, or psychographics. It is because they believe that those characteristics are related to differences in their receptiveness to messages, products, services, ideas, or experiences. Thus, if one were selling a new type of fashionable computer case with anime characters printed on it, one might consider targeting young working women anime fans because they might be most receptive to messages about the product and most likely to purchase it.

The act of choosing a segment to pursue is known as "targeting." The shift away from a message targeted at a mass audience to one tailored to the attention, needs, or interests of a particular subgroup of that mass audience leads to the use of the term "target audience" to describe the intended recipients of these tailored messages. Segmentation and targeting can not only lead to different communication strategies but also to the development of entirely different products or brands. Organizations try to reach a target audience because it is more efficient and effective than trying to reach a mass audience, and the process is evaluated on the basis of the measurability, accessibility, substantiality, and responsiveness of the identified audience.

Hollywood's Target Audience Quadrants

Hollywood insiders tell us that the major studios often use a segmentation scheme to consider the viability of motion pictures or television series, and they are asked to approve or give the "green light."

Their segmentation scheme uses basic demographics (age and gender demographics) to split an audience into four quadrants, which they inaccurately call "quartiles." See Figure 2.2 for a visual representation.

Gender is clearly a dichotomous variable here, and age is arbitrarily split at 25 as if that age signified passing into adulthood. We can think about properties like *John Wick: Chapter 4*, *Ford v Ferrari*, *Billions*, or *Top Gun: Maverick* clearly targeting this so-called first quartile of adult males over the age of 25. Films and TV franchises like *Book Club*, *Wine Country*, *Ocean's 8*, *Big Little Lies*, or *Outlander* are targeted at the second quadrant: adult females over 25 years old. Properties like *Spider-Man: No Way Home* and *Dungeons & Dragons: Honor Among Thieves* and series like *The Mandalorian* and *Cobra Kai* are targeted to the third quadrant of males under the age of 25, while *The Kissing Booth*, *Moxie*, *Set It Up*, *Bridgerton*, and *Taylor Swift: Miss Americana* are targeted to the under-25 females who make up the fourth quadrant.

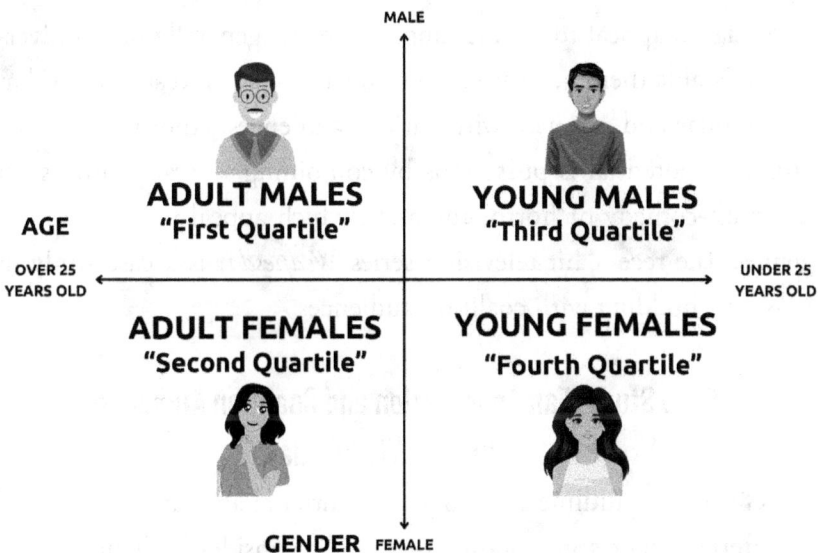

MALE

ADULT MALES "First Quartile"	**YOUNG MALES** "Third Quartile"

AGE

OVER 25 YEARS OLD ← → UNDER 25 YEARS OLD

ADULT FEMALES "Second Quartile"	**YOUNG FEMALES** "Fourth Quartile"

GENDER FEMALE

Figure 2.2: Hollywood's Demographic-Based Quartile Targeting System (source: author-created image).

One of the keys to Hollywood decision-making is whether particular offerings have crossover potential. A film's or other property's crossover potential lies in its perceived ability to appeal to multiple target audience segments. Potential is assessed by exit polls in theaters or by television ratings that split audiences by demographic characteristics. For example, because it balanced a young cast with a well-respected and popular director with a strong record for films, including science fiction, and an established, classic science fiction novel, 2024's *Dune: Part Two* had the crossover potential to attract both young and old audiences, as well as males and females. There was no guarantee it would do so (it did), but it had that potential.

Having crossover potential enhances the perceived commercial viability of a motion picture and is related to the idea of a "blockbuster" or generally appealing entertainment offering. The assessment of a given offering's crossover potential frequently takes place during the development stage and will impact casting decisions, writing choices, and promotional strategies. Motion pictures that have a high potential to appeal to a wide range of people generally have universally relatable themes, a variety of character types, and storylines that are familiar and resonate with various audiences. Another way that crossover potential is pursued is by combining several genres, such as action-comedy or horror-romance, which appeal to fans of both genres. The recent hit television series *Wednesday* is a case study in crossover building with coalition audiences.

Case Study: Fan Aggregation and Coalition Audience Building for Wednesday

Given the unidimensionality of traditional and simplistic forms of entertainment segmentation, we might consider audience strategies based on the fact of the pre-existence of multiple fanships and fandoms. These strategies involve audience gathering and are more related to the logic of fan aggregation than mass audience segmentation. We find them constructed by popular culture-savvy culture producers who understand the inherent potential for multiple, established fandoms to coalesce around new properties that tie into existing relationships. Such a novel model of aggregation and attraction affirms the existence of passionate engagements and weaves them together to form interest in new offerings.

We consider the successful 2022 Netflix television series, *Wednesday*, created by popular filmmaker Tim Burton, to be one such model of an aggregation strategy. The series builds on a long history of fanship of the Charles Addams single-panel comics published in the *New Yorker* from 1938 to 1964, which had been turned into a sitcom, *The Addams Family*, in the 1960s, and had gained an increased following during years of syndication. The same characters inspired two distinct film series: a live-action reboot in the 1990s and a series of animated films beginning in 2019. The characters also appeared in a Broadway musical in 2010. By the time Netflix greenlit or approved it, *The Addams Family* as a franchise had already developed several generations of fans who had followed its comic situations across a range of different media and could thus be expected to know who Wednesday Addams, Morticia, Uncle Fester, and Thing, among other characters were and also to appreciate its unique blend of dark humor and horror.

However, rather than directly soliciting the existing *Addams Family* fan communities, the producers sought to build a series for a new generation of fans—to aggregate multiple groups of fans with different interests—who together formed a coalition audience with crossover target marketing potential. Netflix was among the first to use data and algorithms to find linkages in audience viewing patterns, calculate potential audience demands and develop programs by combining multiple fan interests in a way that tallied them together for market success. Therefore, for example, we can figure that these algorithms were already aware of the number of Tim Burton fans and/or fans of composer Danny Elfman (who enjoyed a long-standing collaboration with Burton), from previous films such as *Beetlejuice*, *Edward Scissorhands* or *The Nightmare Before Christmas*.

We might also point to the rising star status of Jenna Ortega, the Latinx actress who played the younger version of Jane Villanueva in the television series *Jane the Virgin*, and was already recognized by many young fans for her role as the Final Girl in *Scream V* (2022), which was released before the *Wednesday* series launch, as well as *Scream VI* (2023), which was released shortly after its success. It may not have been algorithms that brought Ortega to the screen, but it was likely Burton's popular culture savvy and the casting directors who connected them.

Similarly, consider the links between the Addams Family's dark setting and the popularity of the "school for magic" subgenre, which had gained popularity in America based on the successful *Harry Potter* series and had been deployed with varying degrees of success in *The Descendants*, *School of Good and Evil*, and *Vampire Academy*. The tried-and-tested appeal of the school for magic subgenre would prove the basis for the Nevermore private school on *Wednesday*.

It seems very likely that Netflix determined that there was a significantly larger audience to be found if they triangulated the goth fans who followed Burton's works, the horror and Latinx fans who followed Ortega, and the fantasy enthusiasts who liked the school for magic setting. However, we must recognize that, however scientifically grounded, the aggregation formula does not automatically guarantee commercial success.

Given Netflix's global reach, fans of the property have developed around the world. *Wednesday* was the number one show in 83 countries. Production designer Mark Scruton told *Variety*, "At Nevermore, there's lots of different cultures. You've got gorgons, vampires, sirens, werewolves—it's a melting pot."

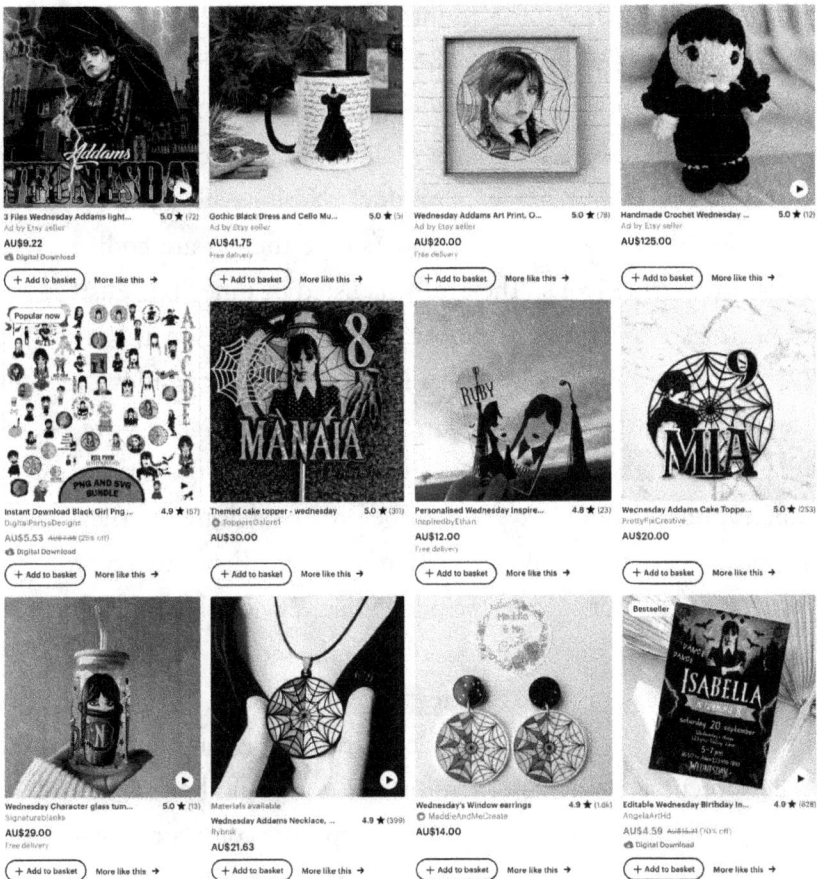

Figure 2.3: Etsy products, listed in December 2024, suggest the persistence of the stained glass window as an iconic image from Netflix's *Wednesday*.

The round, half-color, half-black-and-white stained glass window that was in the room the dark goth, Wednesday, shared with her sparkling and femme roommate, Enid, provided a popular in-group symbol expressing the inclusive melting pot values of the show. The ways that the stained glass window symbolized the bridging of such cultural differences may be what made it such an appealing symbol for fans on contemporary college campuses around the world, similarly shaped by the need to locate a bridge between cultural and subcultural identities. The round window symbol was adopted on Etsy as a theme for grassroots and unauthorized t-shirts, mouse pads, stickers, and iPhone cases, among other merch.

Starting a few months after it aired, we collected several images from Etsy of their *Wednesday* product offerings. This allowed us to trace the process whereby the show's core themes are codified into certain recurring icons. The products listed in June 2023 display the beginnings of a consensus about which elements on the show are of the greatest interest to fans. The stained glass window and the titular character, Wednesday, dressed in full goth gear, were beginning to emerge as favorite reference points for the series. Image 2.3, captured about six months before the release of the second season, suggests how deeply committed the Etsy fan community became to the stained glass window imagery, which persisted as one of the dominant images associated with the series.

Henry wears a shirt that features Wednesday playing her cello in front of the stained glass window. The cello is a reminder of some other potential elements of fan interest that could be mobilized but, in this case, were only done so for the specific community of people who played string instruments (Henry does not, but he likes the shirt anyway). In another franchise, say, *Sherlock*, the character's musical talents might define the character for a larger number of fans.

Figure 2.4: Wednesday Doll on Display in Shanghai (photo © Henry Jenkins).

Henry encountered multiple Wednesday Addams dolls, such as the one pictured in Figure 2.4, during fieldwork in Shanghai, even though, at that point, the Netflix series was not officially available there and could only be viewed through Pirate Bay. The dolls often adopted the character's gothic look and hinted at the series' popular dance moves but never referenced the stained glass window, suggesting that the former's set of connotations may be more pleasurable and meaningful in a Chinese cultural context than the latter.

By skillfully intertwining the nostalgic appeal of *The Addams Family* franchise with contemporary storytelling and fresh faces, Netflix and Tim Burton crafted a series that honors the franchise's almost ninety years of history while effectively inviting in a generation of new fans who were already passionately engaged with adjacent genres and connected characters.

A New Model of Fan Aggregation

This model of what we term "fan aggregation" offers a template for future media productions. It demonstrates a means of bridging generational divides and creating a cohesive viewing experience that leverages shared cultural touchstones in an intelligent way. By aggregating an audience from its fanships and fandoms, metaphorically as well as algorithmically, rather than segmenting it using demographics to split off sections of a mass population, the strategy remains focused on the experience of engagement. It favors wide appeal, like the Dune franchise and *Wednesday*. And it achieves its wide appeal by aggregat-ing different kinds of fan audiences together in complementary, but sometimes surprising, ways.

Burton and Netflix's aggregation strategy may have been rooted in complex data analytics and cultural insights; however, as our next section explains, it also hinges critically on the resonant execution of the content itself. The success of *Wednesday* underscores the potential of an aggregation-type approach to not only preserve the essence of beloved characters and themes but also to innovate and resonate across diverse audience segments.

Wednesday's Earned Fandom

Wednesday was an unprecedented smash hit. During its first week, the series was streamed for 341.2 million hours, more than the prior record holder at the time, *Stranger Things* Season 4. However, to become popular in other senses, it needs to be not simply viewed but also taken up as part of the everyday expressivity of its fans and followers. Within days of its release, one could see other signs of its growing popularity. Ortega allegedly improvised her kooky dance for the show. The dance moves were being widely imitated in YouTube and TikTok videos, including videos where the dance is performed underwater or on ice skates.

Public relations researchers often talk about earned media, referring to the visibility gained because of the autonomous choices made by journalists about what to cover in their publications. In this case, we might think about a concept we call "earned fandom," as fans select from a range of elements on the show that speak to their needs or serve as inspiration for their personal expression. The previously described stained glass window, with its mix of dark and sparkly elements as a signal of bridging across cultural differences, acted as a resonant symbol for those who connected with the series. Many found that it served as an inspiration for their personal expression, just like the dance moves and resulting dance videos from the series did.

Of the potential meanings and pleasures embedded in the crossover hit *Wednesday,* only some of them were activated by audiences, while others fell flat. Even if the producers hoped or anticipated that certain elements might go viral, this is not an arcane science; rather, it depends on the decisions of audience members to activate those symbols within the larger culture. The grassroots appropriations were adopted and amplified by media outlets, such as the number of news stories showcasing various *Wednesday* dance videos or the ways Ortega was invited to perform the dance again on daytime and late-night talk shows. In *Spreadable Media* (Jenkins et al., 2014), Henry and his co-authors make a distinction between the processes of distribution and circulation. Distribution, on the one hand, refers to the top-down, corporately controlled distribution of content. Circulation, on the other hand, refers to the grassroots, networked spread of content. As the example of Wednesday, her stained glass window imagery and her wacky dance illustrate distribution and circulation intersect in complex ways in the contemporary media landscape. People only circulate media that is meaningful to them, and so these moments, where the audience identifies -- and identifies with -- a particular piece of content, like the stained glass window or the dance, help to determine success or failure for producers and brands alike.

Increasingly, the media industries are recognizing the value created through these forms of fan-made materials, which demonstrate fandom's appreciation in two senses: first, in the ways that they perform their love (their appreciation) for certain media properties, and second, in the ways that they appreciate (or increase) their value in the commercial marketplace. Crossover audiences can be powerful when they happen; their translation activities can have synergistic effects that, as they did with *Wednesday*, transmute the enthusiasm of a significant niche audience into mainstream attention.

John Fiske wrote in 1992 that "fans discriminate fiercely; the boundaries between what falls within their fandom and what does not are sharply drawn." (34-35) They discriminate between texts (choosing *Wednesday* over *The School of Good and Evil*, for example) and within texts (choosing the dance scene over other moments in the narrative). Producers often do not know how to predict these forms of fan selectivity. There is a certain human randomness to them that makes their forecasting very difficult. However, the fact of their unpredictability makes it all-important for managers to remain nimble so they can respond quickly to emerging demands and fuel the phenomenon around a cult success property. In fan marketing and fan relations, speed and agility are the order of the day. Our analysis of the success of *Wednesday*, like *Dune* and many other shows and films before them, reveals how a series with a good selection of content, only some of which resonates with the audience, develops a strategy that effectively aggregates disparate existing fanships and fandoms. This is therefore an established pattern for success, if it is not disrupted by other, often diversionary, forces.

Missing the Mark but Hitting the Target

Creating products to meet the consumer needs of a particular target sounds very intentional, as if marketers clearly understand products, their uses, and people's needs and can match them with their own offerings. However, as noted in the sections above, there is a certain human randomness and indeterminacy regarding which elements of a media property will become popular or even whether the entire property will be found appealing.

Occasionally, the fault clearly belongs to marketers, such as when CoverGirl cosmetics promoted the film *The Hunger Games: Catching Fire* with an offering called *The Capitol Collection*. As the Fashionista blog gushed:

> Though the looks created for the film may veer on the extreme side, the Capitol Collection is also ideal for giving your everyday beauty routine an extra shot of Panem-glam. Flamed Up Curl mascara has an extra fluffy tapered wand for a full coverage, thick lashed look, and the six shades of curated Lipslicks Smoochies Sizzle glosses suit pretty much any activity you may embark on—including but not limited to fighting for your life (Crotty, 2014).

Cosmetics suitable for "fighting for your life." Umm... okay. But there is more to the story. The *Hunger Games* is a dystopian story set in Panem, a North American country that has a wealthy

Capitol and 13 districts that exist in varying states of poverty. The use of extreme fashion, which includes over-the-top cosmetics, symbolizes the wealthy Capitol's decadent culture of consumerism and the absurd promotion of superficial trends. These superficial trends, fads, and fashions were necessary to distract the population from the brutal regime that enslaved the outlying districts. It is possible that the managers at CoverGirl intended the line to be a brilliant social critique, for one could easily see the art imitates life elements in the line when you examine the cosmetic collection's beautiful advertising, shown in Figure 2.5. Or perhaps they wanted to promote it as enriched with bitter irony. If not, then they terribly misread the link between cosmetics used in the movie series and the ways its fans might draw meaning and expression from them. We wonder who would not want to proudly wear cosmetics co-branded with District 2's "masonry" and District 10's "livestock" associations?

Figure 2.5: CoverGirl Advertising for The Capitol Collection Tie-in with *The Hunger Games: Catching Fire* Release (circa 2014).

There are numerous examples of products that missed at first but were made successful by their serendipitous adoption by targets other than the ones that were intended or by audiences who came later. Two examples of movies that bombed in their original release but went on to cult success are *The Rocky Horror Picture Show* and *The Room*. Particularly in the arts and with cultural goods, it is not always apparent exactly who might be the intended audience for a particular offering.

Consider Walt Disney's *Fantasia*, a full-length animated motion picture that aimed to fuse classical music with impressionistic animation. The film was very ambitious, expensive to create, and risky. With abstract visuals and challenging musical selections, it was quite unlike prior Disney offerings and, truth be told, Disney had no clear target market in mind. Upon its release in 1940, a difficult time because of World War II, the film was met with a mixed reception. Some critics, accustomed to seeing Disney as a purveyor of folk-inspired popular entertainment, looked down on his foray into "high art." The film's disappointing box-office performance nearly bankrupted Walt Disney Studios and led Disney to regret his lack of a clear target audience.

Nevertheless, despite its initial struggles, *Fantasia* found an enthusiastic new audience among young members of the counterculture movement when it was re-released in the late 1960s. With their embrace of psychedelia and audiovisual experimentation, this new audience was attracted to *Fantasia*'s trippy imagery and musical pairings. College students and young adults flocked to late-night screenings, transforming the film into a cult classic. The newfound popularity led to periodic re-releases, which were key to Disney's revenues for many years, solidifying *Fantasia*'s status first as a counterculture touchstone and now as an undisputed masterpiece of animation.

Target Audiences Beyond Stereotypes

This chapter explains how the concept of "target audience," like the focal concept of "audience" that preceded it, has changed significantly over the decades, reflecting transformations in society, technology, and media. Initially, targeting an audience was tightly coupled with military and governmental strategies that likely followed the focus on mass communication propaganda that was churned out during World War II. This controlled, directive approach to communication did not sit well with the rise of multiple channels of mass media and the recognized rise of an active audience with multiple options. As mass media burgeoned with the rise of radio, television, and later digital platforms, the target audience concept became a fundamental pillar of both marketing and entertainment.

Changes in the target audience concept reflect a social shift towards the recognition of individualism, neoliberalism, consumer choice, and flexible personal identity, trends that distinctly mark the latter half of the 20th century and beyond. As capital markets moved from mass markets to segmented and even individualized markets, marketers and media producers were increasingly forced to view audiences not as a monolithic mass but as one composed of various segments, each with unique preferences and behaviors. However, the view that an audience is composed of segments has problems of its own, as Jim Webster (p. 199) explains:

> All audience studies reduce people to a theoretical abstraction of one sort or another. In conventional audience research, people are typically sorted into a small number of categories (e.g., age, gender, income) and treated as if one person is the functional equivalent of everyone else in the category. Surveys of public opinion introduce additional variables, but take much the same approach.

This stereotyping of segment members is a serious weakness of marketing strategies, a Gordian knot that has never been fully untied. In the world of fan marketing, the tendency to build fictional stereotypes becomes, as we shall see in upcoming chapters, too great to resist. When we consider the passionate and collective engagement of members of fandoms, segmentation strategies that do not seriously build on elements of participatory culture miss a golden opportunity to turn traditional marketing on its head. Instead of dictating terms, marketers must find ways to collaborate and dialogue with fandoms and their members, just as they are still learning how to do so in relation to the influencer economy and its many important offshoots. The phenomenon of "earned fandom" highlights this shift. The choices that fans and members of fandoms make can not only amplify a product's success or consign it to obscurity; however, they can also contribute powerful and lasting innovation and insight.

Moreover, the unpredictable nature of fandom highlights the limits of traditional market forecasting based on current understandings of target audiences. It would be a serious mistake to assume that the set of fan-related psychographic characteristics that one is able to map onto a group of Japanese females between 18–25 years old in 2020 are the same as those that will match those same Japanese females today. Contexts are continually changing, and people are with them. Tracking that same generation of Japanese females will reveal that their tastes have changed just as the social, political, cultural, technological, family, institutional, and other elements of their world have changed. Trying to map those old characteristics onto a new generation of Japanese women will turn out to be just as futile. The dynamism of contexts and people means that simple and convenient segmentation schemes like Hollywood's quartiles are deeply problematic tools.

However, all is not lost. Context change can turn supposed winners into losers, but it can just as easily turn losers into winners. Just as *Fantasia* initially missed its mark upon its original release but later found an unexpected audience, many cultural productions may find their success in ways unanticipated by their creators. This unpredictability is not a sign of poor marketing but a fact of contemporary life. It is also a call for contemporary marketing and public relations to constantly build new levels of nimbleness and flexibility. One way to do this would be by partnering with small, entrepreneurial, and possible fan- and fandom-owned producers of different kinds. Products like *Wednesday* not only need to meet the existing tastes of their target demographics but also resonate on a more profound, subcultural, and perhaps even subconscious level with emergent and sometimes unforeseeable contexts.

The role of crossover potential in these anticipate-the-unanticipatable processes cannot be overstated. The ability of a motion picture, series, or product to appeal to multiple demographic, psychographic, geographic, or behavioral segments can spell the difference between a niche success that satisfies a few thousand people and a breakout hit that manages to ride a massive wave of success, reaching millions. These qualities of crossover flexibility are achieved not through clever communications but through engineering meaningful cultural connections into the cultural product itself—its thematic richness, relatability, and the universal appeal of its core story, values, and the imagined world it summons. Whether blending musical genres, emphasizing sports franchise histories, strategically casting actors, or incorporating universally engaging themes into video games, a proper and appropriate balance of these universal dramatic elements (not a messy mishmash of them) holds the potential to enhance the appeal of cultural productions to broader audiences.

AI Obsoleting Traditional Segmentation Practices

The rise of AI in fan marketing might signal the pending obsolescence of traditional audience segmentation practices. AI's capacity to analyze huge amounts of data and then tailor marketing efforts to individuals rather than to groups ushers in the era of true "markets of one." In this brave new market, segmentation—a cornerstone of marketing strategy—becomes an endangered species as personalization reaches new, unprecedented levels. Intriguingly, this shift parallels innovations in media personalization, such as "choose your own adventure" narratives like the episode "Bandersnatch" in Netflix's *Black Mirror*. Remarkably, that episode had five possible endings and over a trillion possible permutations! Audiences of the episode end up watching very different shows as they navigate their own individualized paths.

Such interactivity hints at a future where media content itself becomes increasingly fragmented, enabling viewers to experience customized versions of shows. For example, perhaps a future season of *Bridgerton* will allow viewers to choose their preferred romantic pairing. Perhaps *Star Wars* fans will be able to generate their own new episodes or series. The origin story of R2D2? Deeper background on Han Solo's love life as a teen? (We actually got too much of it later in *Solo*). No problem! Just as AI now generates images and short videos, it may soon generate entire television shows or motion pictures from single prompts. This potential hyper-personalization challenges the scalability of traditional storytelling while also blurring the line between creator-driven narratives and consumer co-creation. For marketers, this evolution amplifies the need to rethink strategies, emphasizing responsiveness and adaptability to cater to uniquely tailored fan experiences while still attempting to keep in mind the emotional, social, and passionate responses of audience members.

Although the concept of the target audience originated from a propagandistic need to control and direct, it continues to suggest new mechanisms that may eventually lead to more profound engagement, understanding, and mutual influence between culture producers and their audiences. As we shift back and forth from marketing's control mechanisms and the agentic counter-responses of engaged audiences, this tension between culture's expressive impulse and commodification's need to suppress and monetize them increasingly demands our attention. The next chapter delves into this central topic by introducing and then building upon foundational concepts of culture that have been highly influential in the field of fandom studies.

CHAPTER 3:

The Audience is "Ordinary"

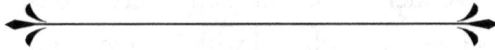

As we transition from considering the ways media industries seek to capture and capitalize on fan engagement, we now shift our focus to the cultural underpinnings of fan behavior. While marketing experts primarily view fans as consumers, this chapter explores how fandoms introduce various cultural backgrounds, identities, and interpretations into their media experiences. Moving beyond the market logic of segmentation, we will examine how fans' cultural investments shape not only how they engage with media but also how they infuse media with new meanings and purposes.

Raymond Williams' foundational work, "Culture is Ordinary" (Williams, 1989), sets the stage for this exploration by challenging the notion of culture as something exclusive and elite. Williams emphasizes that culture is woven into the fabric of everyday life, shaping how people—fans included—experience, interpret, and respond to media. This understanding informs how fans bring their cultural contexts and struggles into their interpretations. We use Clifford Geertz's analysis of cockfighting in Bali (Geertz, 1994) and Robert Darnton's study of the "Great Cat Massacre" (Darnton, 1984) to elucidate how ethnographically informed accounts strive to understand the complex practices that may seem obvious and ordinary to those enacting them. Fan activities reflect similarly deep-seated and difficult-to-decipher cultural meanings. In addition, fans' critical engagement with media often highlights the complexities of their lived reality, such as tensions around representation, including regarding race, gender, class, and their intersections, as well as how these identities intersect with and within fan communities.

Defining Culture

Matthew Arnold (1869) on Culture:

The whole scope of the essay is to recommend culture as the great help out of our present difficulties; culture being a pursuit of our total perfection by means of getting to know, on all the matters which most concern us, the best which has been thought and said in the world, and, through this knowledge, turning a stream of fresh and free thought upon our stock notions and habits, which we now follow staunchly but mechanically, vainly imagining that there is a virtue in following them staunchly which makes up for the mischief of following them mechanically (p. iii).

Raymond Williams (1989) on Culture:

Culture is ordinary: that is the first fact. Every human society has its own shape, its own purposes, its own meanings. Every human society expresses these, in institutions and in arts and learning. The making of a society is the finding of common meanings and directions, and its growth is an active debate and amendment under the pressures of experience, contact, and discovery, writing itself into the land (p.93).

What Do We Mean by Culture?

Rather than thinking of media audiences as blank slates onto which media producers and brand managers project their images, we might recognize audiences as always being a part of a larger culture that they bring with them—whether into the movie theater, sports arena, grocery store, or amusement park. These pre-existing cultural investments frame how they understand the cultural products they are engaging with.

The roots of fandom studies can be found in the work of the Centre for Contemporary Cultural Studies (CCCS) at the University of Birmingham, UK (often described as the Birmingham School). Along with the historian E. P. Thompson, the literary critic Richard Hogarth, and the theorist Stuart Hall, the

Welsh-born critic and novelist Raymond Williams is widely acknowledged as one of the founders of the cultural studies approach. More than any other piece of writing, William's "Culture is Ordinary" (1989) set the tone for the British Cultural Studies movement. Williams offers a more inclusive model of culture, a concept Williams would describe more fully in *Keywords* (1976). William's conception of culture contrasts with that of 19th-century cultural critic Matthew Arnold.

Clifford Geertz (1973) on Culture:

Believing, with Max Weber, that man is an animal suspended in webs of significance he himself has spun; I take culture to be those webs and the analysis of it to be, therefore, not an experimental science in search of law but an interpretive one in search of meaning. It is explication I am after, construing social expressions on their surface enigmatical... The concept of culture I espouse... is essentially a semiotic one (p. 5).

Culture is public because meaning is (p. 12).

Arnold's approach was exclusive: only a very narrow selection of things, "the best" could be considered "culture," and only a small number of people could be considered "cultured," a metaphor drawn from agriculture where it originally referred to the cultivation of the land or the human transformation of the environment. William's approach is expansive, embracing the arts and the sciences, the exceptional and the ordinary, the traditional and the emergent. For Williams, culture is at once the stuff of learning, an acquired set of skills and appreciations, and the stuff of experience, part of the daily lives of ordinary folks.

Williams—then in his late 20s—opened the debate in 1958 with a blistering manifesto for a new approach, "Culture Is Ordinary." Perhaps the essay's most radical element is the way Williams pits his own lived experience growing up working class in the Welsh countryside against what his own mentors were teaching him at Cambridge: "When the Marxists say that we live in a dying culture and that the masses are ignorant, I have to ask them, as I did ask them, where on Earth they have lived. A dying culture, and ignorant masses are not what I have known and see" (p. 96). Cultural studies commit themselves to better understanding the ongoing struggle over what counts as culture and who gets to decide what culture matters.

Williams is at his most moving when he describes what reading and writing meant for his family: "My grandfather, a big hard laborer, wept while he spoke, finely and excitedly, at the parish meeting" (p. 92), he tells us, while his father, a labor organizer, read through the lines of news stories to identify entrenched economic interests. He talks about the value his people placed on library books and states that many more would have gone to college except for the financial responsibilities they bore to their families and their communities. He describes a visit home after his time in college and discusses the tension he felt within himself as he looked at their culture through eyes shaped by formal education:

> Now they read, they watch this work we are talking about: some of them quite critically, some with a great deal of pleasure. Very well, I read different things, watch different entertainments, and I am quite sure why they are better... But talking to my family, to my friends, talking, as we were, about our own lives, about people, about feelings, could I, in fact, find this lack of quality we are discussing? I'll be honest -- I looked; my training has done this for me. I can only say that I found as much natural fitness of feeling, as much quick discrimination, as much clear grasp of ideas within that range of experiences as I have found anywhere. (Williams, 1989, p. 99)

As with many people, receiving an elite higher education changed how he saw the culture of his upbringing, which suggests a more dynamic sense of culture that shapes William's vision. Culture is not a static collection of texts, as it seems to be for Arnold, but rather a set of everyday practices and assumptions that change in relation to the world around it.

Williams (1989) contrasts this sense of a community eagerly engaged in conversation with the snootiness of the tea shop just outside his university, which taught him in the most painful way possible that some see culture as "the outward and emphatically visible sign of a special kind of people." (p. 93) Williams (1989) suggests, "If this is culture, we don't want it." (p. 93) Much of what Williams encountered in the tea shop is what we today would refer to as "microaggressions," commonplace disdainful expressions or behavior towards someone because of their race, ethnicity, gender, sexuality, disability or social standing designed to make them feel like they do not belong. People compare microaggressions to bee stings: one by itself may only hurt a bit, but a day-to-day barrage of many such stings can cause lasting damage.

Through such images, Williams (1989, p. 96) conveys his discomfort with the policing of cultural boundaries, the ranking of cultural products, and the dismissal of other people's cultures. While himself critical of the "cheapjack" quality of the new industrially produced culture, Williams articulates a great distrust of the "directive" impulse in the intellectuals who seek to "impose" their cultural assumptions on the unlearned masses. "There are no masses, but ways of seeing people as masses," Williams (ibid) writes in a statement that is a profound critique of the audience-as-mass viewpoint provided above. He also distrusts the anti-intellectual impulses in his own background, the ways that working class critics dismiss "culture vultures" and "do gooders," even when doing so cuts them off from resources that might improve the quality of their lives. Something vital is at stake in these struggles over culture, and his goal as an educator was to help people better articulate their own cultural politics.

Although there is no explicit evidence that Raymond Williams directly influenced the American anthropologist Clifford Geertz, it is highly plausible that Geertz was aware of Williams' work and that it certainly contributed to the broader intellectual climate in which Geertz's ideas developed. Both Geertz and Williams were prominent figures in the "cultural turn" of the mid-20th century, a period marked by a renewed focus on the importance of culture and meaning in various academic disciplines. Their work also shared some key similarities: they both emphasized meaning, rejected simple dichotomies, preached keen attention to context, and distanced themselves from purely descriptive or structuralist approaches to culture while emphasizing the importance of understanding the meanings and values people attach to their practices. They both disputed simplistic distinctions between "high" and "low" culture while recognizing the complicated interpenetration of different forms and expressions of culture, and both scholars highlighted the need to situate cultural phenomena within their historical and social contexts. Other scholars, including Yilena Reyes (2024), have noted the connections between Williams and Geertz on what constitutes contemporary culture.

Cocks and Cats, Oh My!

Henry here. Clifford Geertz (1994) was responsible for one of the two essays I most often ask my students to read as examples of cultural analysis: Geertz's "Notes on a Balinese Cock Fight" and historian Robert Darnton's "The Great Cat Massacre," both discuss the question of popular amusements. Due to their focus on activities that harm animals, both essays can potentially strike a nerve; the activities they describe are alien and disturbing in a modern Western context. That is part of the point: to use cultural analysis to unlock meaning in things we consider meaningless or unacceptable. Therefore, you should suspend judgment.

Geertz's essay begins with an account of the process of how he, as an outsider and an ethnographer, became accepted by the community he sought to study, culminating in a moment when he and his wife fled with the Balinese locals from a police raid on a cockfight. He writes, "The next morning, the village was a completely different world for us. Not only were we no longer invisible, but we were also suddenly the center of all attention, the object of a great outpouring of warmth, interest, and, most especially, amusement. Everyone in the village knew we had fled like everyone else" (Geertz, 1994, p. 98).

Fan Culture

Williams' ideas have influenced fandom studies in several important ways. First, he empowered those who followed him to explore their own cultural lives and to examine forms of cultural expression that had been excluded from academic view. This broader set of notions regarding what constitutes culture leads from the consideration of flamboyant street cultures, such as punks, teddy boys, and goths, to fan communities. We discuss this transition in **Fandom as Subculture**. William's defense of the importance of studying his own cultural identity and experience continues to pave the way for every other person who may be a first generation college student, comes from a background that has not traditionally been factored into the university experience, or otherwise feels marginalized and minoritized.

Second, cultural studies as an approach dismisses the idea that popular culture—and, by extension, the fan communities that grew up around it—is "meaningless." We, as humans, are constantly involved in meaning-making and, because of

Here, we see how Geertz addresses issues of positionality in his study of this sporting practice, shifting from outsider to uneasy insider, and thus, how he negotiated his relationship with his object of study. In **Fandom as a Subculture**, we consider the debates around positionality that have shaped fandom studies as a particular form of participant observation.

Throughout "Notes on a Balinese Cock Fight," Geertz takes us deeper and deeper into what he describes as "the deep psychological identification of Balinese men with their cocks" (p. 99) (pun intended by Geertz). He explores how the Balinese men decide where to place their bets based on kinship and other social relations. Geertz also discusses the emotional front they construct when they lose, often much more than they can afford to sacrifice. He sums it up as, "In the cockfight, man and beast, good and evil, ego and id, the creative power of aroused masculinity and the destructive power of loosened animality fuse in a bloody drama of hatred, cruelty, violence, and death" (p. 101).

Whatever readers think of cockfighting as an activity (personally, we find it immensely cruel), Geertz helps us to understand what it means to those who participate, working us from a state of discomfort and distance towards one of greater understanding. Geertz himself refers to this process of layered analysis as "thick description" as he untangles how a popular activity fits into the culture around it. His descriptions are vivid and intense; he cares about the particulars, but he does not leave it there—he continues to dig deeper into the cultural logic of this form of "deep play" and how it may elucidate cultural analysis more generally. Near the end, he turns his attention to the ways that the cockfight functions as an art form:

> As any art form—for that, finally, is what we are dealing with -the cockfight renders ordinary, everyday experience comprehensible.... What it does is what, for other peoples with other temperaments and other conventions, Lear and Crime and Punishment do; it catches up these themes—death, masculinity, rage, pride, loss, beneficence, chance— and ordering them into an encompassing structure, presents them in such a way as to throw into relief a particular view of their essential nature (pp. 117-118).

In the same way professional wrestling may be a meaningful form of expression for its fans, even if it is, as they are so often and so rudely reminded, "fake," the cockfight, Geertz argues, may be a meaningful form of expression, even though it is "real" (at least to the birds). Here, Geertz returns to a core principle in cultural studies: the idea that if we do not understand what an activity means to its participants, then it is our obligation to investigate, listen, and learn.

Geertz's writing inspired cultural historian Robert Darnton to apply the tools of cultural analysis to examine popular entertainment practices of the past. We consider another of Darnton's essays about Rousseau and his readers this, tend not to engage in activities that are meaningless.

The researcher may not understand why a particular practice is meaningful to those who engage with it; however, that just means the researcher needs to dig deeper and immerse themselves more fully in the community for whom the practice is meaningful, as Geertz and Darnton did. While Rob and Henry are fans, no one could be a fan of the full range of examples we discuss in this book. Therefore, our methodology combines self-reflection with ethnographic and empathetic investigation and a strong reliance on insights from secondary literature.

At the heart of Raymond Williams' scholarship is a challenge to established cultural norms and hierarchies that inform how we can consider fans and consumers. His work highlighted how dominant media narratives, often controlled by a select few, shape our perceptions and create societal stereotypes. By critiquing these narratives, Williams paved the way for a more democratic understanding of culture, one that factors in the importance of including diverse voices, experiences, and perspectives. As a result, we are drawn to question the way that various acts of consumption—such as being a nerdy science fiction fan, a lovesick Harry Styles fan, a first-person video game shooter player, or a testerone-pumped metalhead—force us to consider which groups have the power to deem some forms of consumption excessive or unacceptable. Each of the above examples suggests an anxiety about taking cultural works too seriously (being nerdy), about becoming too emotional (becoming "lovesick"), or about the potential threat of performing fictional gestures in the real world. Gender norms may also enter these representations in the form of anxiety about men displaying excessive emotion at concerts or women consuming media intended for male audiences.

Williams also emphasized the importance of understanding media consumers not as a monolithic entity but as a collection of diverse audiences, subcultures, and publics. His work is less focused on the audience as a mass, and more on the concept of the audience as an agent. His work underscores the idea that

in **Fandom as Desire**. In "The Great Cat Massacre" (Darnton, 1984), he is interested in a 'comic' incident where a group of French workers rounded up several cats, including their mistress's pet, and killed them, an incident they—though clearly not their mistress—found hysterically funny. Darnton seeks to understand why. As he writes,

> Our own inability to get the joke is an indication of the distance that separates us from the workers of preindustrial Europe… Anthropologists have found that the best points of entry in an attempt to penetrate an alien culture can be those where it seems to be most opaque. When you realize that you are not getting something… that is particularly meaningful to the natives, you can see where to grasp a foreign system of meaning in order to unravel it (p. 78).

Modeling his work on Geertz's "thick description" approach, Darnton models many layers of analysis, proposing multiple contexts for understanding why this act of petty revenge on a domineering boss was comic for those who performed this disturbing act, including sexual puns about pussies and femininity as blunt as those Geertz made around cocks and masculinity.

Certainly, many readers will be uncomfortable encountering the essay's discussion of the abuse of domestic animals or the casual misogyny of the French workmen, so be forewarned. However, what also remains with me from this essay (and the reason that it matters to us) is the call to dig deeper to understand the laughter of past cultures. These essays offer us a model for the type of work required to conduct cultural analysis correctly, as well as what it might take to understand another group's fandom.

media consumption is not a one-size-fits-all phenomenon. Different groups interact with media in different ways, bringing with them their unique backgrounds, experiences, and interpretations. This nuanced understanding highlights the richness and diversity of media audiences and allows for a more comprehensive analysis of their behaviors, motivations, and beliefs.

Furthermore, Williams draws our attention to the role and position of the researcher in studying fan and brand communities. Rather than being a detached observer who somehow checks their fan interest or consumer self at the door, the researcher is considered to be inherently tied to the subject of study, bringing their perspectives and experiences into the analysis. Recognizing this positionality is crucial because it highlights the power dynamics at work in research and emphasizes the importance of researcher reflexivity. We will return to this issue in **Fandom as Subculture**, where we consider Angela McRobbie, another Birmingham school researcher.

As Henry Jenkins (2007) argues, popular culture demands an emotional investment from those of us who consume it. If the researcher stays emotionless and distant (a stance that sometimes passes itself off as "objective"), they can never fully understand their object of study. To research fandom, it is not necessary to be a fan; however, it sure helps, and the majority of fandom studies scholars are. Nevertheless, the ability to examine your own stakes in popular culture while also giving yourself over to affective relations with its materials is necessary, at least at the moment, as empathy for the fan community under study develops.

Henry recalls a professor he had in graduate school who told their students that they should "always write about things they hate because this was the only way to get sufficient critical distance from them." However, hate, like love, is an emotional perspective and the opposite of objectivity. Hate <u>can</u> lead to insights; nonetheless, it is not the only way, and it is a psychically draining way to live, especially when compared with the joy that comes from integrating work and pleasure.

Many media and fan scholars have followed Williams' legacy and adopted a political stance that remains critical of dominant institutions, including media corporations. There is a recognition that these institutions often serve vested interests by perpetuating various narratives to maintain the status quo and those who benefit from it. By adopting a skeptical view of media messaging and its power imbalances, researchers can uncover biases and provide alternative narratives that are more inclusive and representative of the diversity of media audiences. Furthermore, this skepticism translates into support for organic grassroots fan and brand organizations, recognizing their power and agency to shape media narratives and challenge the dominant ideologies of the hegemony. The debates within the Birmingham School resurface in **Fandom as Subculture** and **Fandom as Public**.

Yet another enduring contribution of Williams' scholarship is the emphasis on understanding everyday life, particularly through the lenses of gender, sexuality, race, class, and nationality. These are not mere categories but are foundational concepts that shape our experiences, identities, and interactions with the world. In the context of fan culture, these various cornerstones become crucial. Fans are not homogenous; they bring with them diverse identities, which influence their connections, interpretations, and contributions to fan culture. By focusing on these aspects, researchers can highlight issues of representation, power, and agency in fan and consumer behaviors.

Today's fandom studies push beyond an understanding of these categories in isolation, and instead, many researchers are interested in models of intersectionality as proposed by critical legal scholar

Kimberle Crenshaw. Crenshaw (2013) sought to understand bias and discrimination, suggesting that her experience as a Black woman was accumulative; she suffered discrimination as someone who was both Black and female and, therefore, those experiences would necessarily differ from the experiences of Black men, White women, or White men. This focus on intersectionality is forcing fandom studies to be ever more precise about which fans we are discussing and what cultural experiences shape the forms of fandom they embrace.

Frames of Fandom will continue to consider each of these aspects and questions as we consider how contemporary fandom studies took shape and why extensive fandom studies literature mat-ters. Stuart Hall, for example, sharpened the Birmingham School's focus on television audiences and how they decoded semiotic texts. This focus would lead first to more ethnographic approaches to audience research and, ultimately, to fandom studies.

Cultural Ordinariness and Global Fandoms Today

We can see how Raymond Williams' and other theoretical views of culture as 'ordinary' permeate into global fandoms today, which hold increasingly important roles and act as centers of power and influence within contemporary consumer culture. The assertion that culture is rooted in the everyday resonates strongly with the phenomenon of fandoms transforming ordinary objects, media, and historical artifacts into important and lasting sites of meaning, nostalgia, and identity. This cultural ordinariness is linked to the shared values and historical contexts that give rise to many collective practices and affinities. For example, the resurgence of nostalgia-driven fandoms, such as the "Ostalgie" movement in post-reunification Germany, reflects how everyday objects from East Germany's DDR era, which were once viewed as functional or mundane, have become fetishized artifacts symbolizing a desirable and lost cultural identity (Brunk, Giesler, and

Hartmann, 2018). These items, ranging from Trabant cars to Spreewald pickles, evoke not only nostalgia but also subtle resistance to dominant narratives of capitalist triumphalism.

Similarly, the success of mysterious Detroit-based 70's rock icon Sixto Rodriguez during Apartheid South Africa highlights the power of fandom to challenge geopolitical and cultural boundaries. His music, originally relegated to obscurity in his home country (United States), became a rallying point for South African listeners who used it as a soundtrack for subtle resistance against an oppressive regime (Hylsop, 2013). This grassroots canonization of an artist illustrates how fandom can coalesce around shared cultural values, even under restrictive political systems, underscoring the complex interplay between culture, politics, and consumption.

In Brazil, the enduring popularity of *Chaves*, a Brazilian Portuguese-dubbed version of the cartoon Mexican television sitcom *El Chavo del Ocho*, reflects how humor and relatability transcend geographic and linguistic barriers. Despite initial resistance by studios and skepticism regarding the ability of the show's humor to translate from Mexico to Brazil, the show became a cornerstone of Brazilian pop culture. The Brazilian Portuguese dub was broadcast by the Brazilian channel SBT and its affiliates almost without interruption for more than 36 years, from 1984 to 2020. In 2003, it went off the air for a short period of 10 days but had to be reinstated after angry protests from fans (de Carvalho, Marques, and Frangella, 2017).

Similarly, in the Middle East, the rise of fandoms surrounding Turkish soap operas such as *Gümüş* (*Noor* in Arabic) demonstrates how narratives steeped in family values and emotional intensity are recontextualized by Arab audiences to reflect their cultural ideals and social conversations and have subsequently risen to become an impressive form of diplomatic soft power respected throughout the region (Buccianti, 2010).

In Austria, Wickie, Slime & Paiper Clubbing-West exemplify how fandom can transform the everyday into a cult (Horak, 2006). These club events, rooted in 1970s and 1980s cultural nostalgia, celebrate an era through fashion, music, and even commodities, such as the reintroduced Paiper ice cream. By reviving this tasty and nostalgic food product, the Unilever subsidiary Eskimo successfully tapped into a market fueled by emotional connection and collective memory, demonstrating how fandom-driven culture can work in concert with astute corporate management to read and ride the cultural waves of popular consumption patterns.

These global examples demonstrate how audiences become dynamic interpreters and co-creators, refashioning ordinary artifacts into symbols of shared identity and meaning. In the wake of these processes of reinterpretation, consumer movements redefine and revive the ordinary. Through collective actions, such as themed events or social media campaigns, they elevate artifacts—whether a television series, a product, or a historical moment—into cultural touchstones. This revival is often entwined with economic impacts as industries reintroduce products or tailored content that responds to these trends in taste, reinforcing the already intimate feedback loops between culture and commerce. Transforming the everyday into reservoirs of meaning, these fandoms establish new cultural and economic networks. They not only reshape how brands engage with consumers but also enrich cultural narratives, demonstrating the enduring applicability of Williams' concept of culture as ordinary in a globalized, participatory world.

CHAPTER 4:

Decoding the Audience

The Encoding/Decoding Model

As we move beyond Raymond Williams' assertion that culture is ordinary to a more focused examination of how media messages are received and interpreted, we shift from viewing audiences as culturally situated participants to exploring the ways that their meaning-making activities express and create that cultural situation. Stuart Hall's (1973) work was one of the first and most forceful challenges to the notion that audiences passively absorb media messages. Instead, Hall revealed a far more intriguing process.

Building on the notion that culture is shaped by everyday life and intersecting identities, this chapter will delve into how audience members, who are embedded in their own social contexts, decode media in ways that reflect both personal and collective struggles for meaning. Just as Williams (1976) emphasized that culture is contested and lived, Hall's work on hegemony and interpretation demonstrates that audiences play a crucial role in shaping the cultural power relations around them.

Stuart Hall's essay, "Encoding, Decoding," first published in 1973, sought an integrated model of the communication process, one that considered production, circulation, use, and reproduction. It was his response to simpler signal sender and receiver models, like Claude Shannon and Warren Weaver's (1948) theory, which saw the role of the audience primarily as recovering the intended message of its producer and saw a deviation from the recovery of authorial meaning in terms of audience 'failure' and 'noise' disrupting the 'signal.'

Elsewhere, Hall (1981) rejects, on the one hand, the idea that the people are simply dupes of a powerful media industry and, on the other, what he describes as the "heroic alternative" to a "whole, authentic, autonomous" popular culture outside "cultural power and domination" (p. 512). Rather, Hall writes:

> "Popular culture is one of the sites where this struggle for and against a culture of the powerful is engaged: it is also the stake to be won or lost in that struggle. It is the arena of consent and resistance. It is partially where hegemony arises and where it is secured" (Hall, 1981, p. 518).

Hegemony refers to a particular theory of ideological contestation, arising from the work of Italian Marxist Antonio Gramsci in his *Prison Notebooks (Quaderni del carcere)* (1975), which imagines a dynamic and ongoing struggle over meaning and interpretation between the dominant sectors of society and the people, the workers, the subordinate classes (Hall, 2016).

Here is how Hall (1980) talks about the encoding process for television: "The institutional structures of broadcasting, with their practices and networks of production, their organized relations and technical infrastructures, are required to produce a programme... In one sense, then, the circuit begins here" (p. 128). Hall explored the ways that the encoding process is shaped by a range of "knowledge-in-use concerning the routines of production, historically defined technical skills, professional ideologies, institutional knowledge, definitions and assumptions, assumptions about the audience and so on" (ibid). He also suggested the ways that what gets produced functions in conversation with other sources from which "they draw topics, treatments, agendas, events, personnel, images of the audience... definitions of the situation" (ibid).

Today, the "encoding" process (production) remains mostly in the domain of production studies, while what Hall calls "use" (reception) and "reproduction" (how audiences respond once they "decode" a text)—and in more recent work, grassroots "circulation" (Jenkins, Ford, and Green, 2013)—constitutes fandom or audience studies. Drawing on semiotics, Hall describes the ways that social codes (often unexamined assumptions) inform choices about what content to produce, circulate, consume, and reproduce. As Hall (1980) explains, "Once accomplished, the discourse must then be translated—transformed, again—into social practices if the circuit is to be both completed and effective.

Audience "Activation"

In marketing and targeted communication—whether for-profit brands, public health initiatives, political campaigns, or nonprofit organizations seeking donations—the concept of target audience "activation" is often considered central. The focus of marketing communication is not on communication for its own sake but on driving an action of one sort or another. Marketers and other communicators, therefore, design their messages with specific and measurable goals in mind: getting someone to donate, purchase, click, sign up, or engage in some specified way. This goal is often achieved through carefully composed and placed "calls to action" (CTAs), which prompt the audience to take immediate steps, whether it is making a purchase, scheduling an appointment, or signing a petition.

For public health communicators, audience activation might mean encouraging a healthier lifestyle by promoting flu shots or vaccinations. For nonprofits, the goal could be donations or volunteer sign-ups. Political campaigns aim to motivate their audiences of voters to take action. Those actions could include attending rallies, donating, or casting their ballots. In every case, the communication strategy is built around fluidly moving people from receiving information to acting on it and contributing to the communicator's desired outcome.

It turns out that audience activation is comparable to sales. Activation strategies include ubiquitous CTAs, urgency and emotional appeals, incentives, celebrity endorsements, and clear, direct messaging, all designed to provoke a response, often an immediate one. For example, limited-time offers or donation matches are commonly used to create a sense that swift action is required, compelling the audience to act now rather than later. Rarely, if ever, are these communications created without a clear goal tied to behavior change or action. Whether it is to drive sales, promote health behaviors, or mobilize political support, the ultimate measure of communication success lies in the actions taken because of the message—this is the essence of activation. In short, producers and marketers want active, not passive, audiences.

But we must also consider Raymond Williams' (1976) view that language is important and that words' meanings are often political and powerful. How might we compare the concept of "activation" in the marketing field with the notion of active audience in the cultural studies literature? What does it mean to say that an audience is "activated" by a marketer? Do statements such as these deprive the audience of agency and provide it solely to the advertiser? Does the term invite a manipulative attitude? Are audiences passive and disengaged until they are activated by some outside force?

We believe that we must be cautious when using terms such as "activation" to refer to how we view and treat other human beings—a theme we return to when we consider brand communities in **Fandom as Consumer Collective**.

If no 'meaning' is taken, there can be no 'consumption.' If the meaning is not articulated in practice, it has no effect" (Hall, 1980, p. 128).

The field of fandom studies nowadays primarily concentrates on the moment of "reproduction" or re-production, where fans act upon the decoded message in some way; however, the majority of Hall's "Encoding, Decoding" (1980) deals with the moment of reception as the audience decodes the discourse and interprets the story of the television program. This focus on reproduction signals a recognition that the cycle of communication does not end, that fans are often not only readers of existing texts but producers of new ones, and that fans often try to signal back to the producer their desires and interests so they may inform the next cycle of production.

Building on the concept of hegemony, Hall (1980) describes the ways different consumers relate to mass media messages: some read them fully within the terms of the dominant ideology, while others resist or reject them outright. However, many will negotiate, taking them apart and taking part in them in equal measure because the intended meanings are imperfectly aligned with their experiences. "Decoding within the negotiated position contains a mixture of adaptive and oppositional elements: it acknowledges the legitimacy of the hegemonic definitions to make the grand significations (abstract), while, at a more restricted, situational (situated) level, it makes its own ground rules—it operates with exceptions to the rule" (p. 137).

Henry recalls the experience of watching the movie *The Towering Inferno* (1974) with his father, who was a building inspector. His father had no trouble imagining contractors trying to cut corners in the construction of the building. Still, he had much greater faith in the ability of inspectors to spot such mistakes and thus prevent the disaster from happening. His critique of corporate greed was limited in this case by his faith in the part of the system where he operated.

It is important that these responses be understood as "negotiated readings" rather than "negotiating readers," since the same viewer may be oppositional to some texts, negotiate with others, or accept the preferred meanings in yet other cases. These are relationships between readers and texts, not classes of readers. When the field of Fandom Studies launched in the 1990s, fans were often described as "resistant readers," though increasingly, we have come to understand their dominant practices as forms of negotiation. Such readers have agency; however, they do not have autonomy; various forms of power shape the meanings they can assert. Such readers embrace textual elements they recognize and value, but there are problematic aspects that produce discomfort that have to be addressed before fans can claim ownership over these representations. Each of us is positioned somewhat differently in relation to dominant representations, negotiating different identities and identifications within ourselves (as Hall 1992b notes). However, those whose gender, class, racial, and sexual identities fall within dominant groups find it easiest to forge identifications with mass media texts: they are the recipients the producers anticipated. Hall describes certain interpretations as "dominant" or "preferred" but not "determined" in that any given audience may have access to multiple "codes" or "framings" through which they might make sense of a textual element: "It is always possible to order, classify, assign and decode an event within more than one 'mapping'" (p. 131).

Negotiating with *Harry Potter*

Henry (Jenkins, 2017) has written a case study of *Harry Potter* fans who have generated a reading of the books where the character Hermione Granger is portrayed as Black or of a Mixed ethnic background ("Mudblood") and shown how this approach emerged through their ongoing negotiations with the text, its author, and with each other to find a place for themselves within books they love but incorporate few characters of color. The author of the *Harry Potter* series, J.K. Rowling, has since claimed that she left open the possibility for a Black Hermione by including few descriptive details of the character beyond kinky hair and, in one passage, brownish skin. Similarly, a Black actress was cast in the part in the original West End production of *Harry Potter and the Cursed Child* in 2016.

Henry focused his analysis on a post made on *BuzzFeed* in 2015 by Alanna Bennett, who characterized herself as a "mixed race" fan of Hermione Granger. She wrote:

> I related to her deeply but like with so much of what I watched and read, I couldn't see myself in Hermione. There was a gap, and even for a kid as obsessed with pop culture as I was, it was one that existed between me

and most of the things I was reading and watching…
In *Harry Potter and the Sorcerer's Stone*, Hermione is
introduced with a description of her bushy brown hair
and her large teeth. There's nothing there to indicate
she didn't look just like me, yet I always pictured a
white face under that bushy head. I always pictured her
not-me. (NP)

Her conflicted and ambivalent sense of identification with a
character who was simultaneously "not me" was a classic example of what Hall meant by "negotiated reading," an impossible
fantasy that the media representation of this character might be
otherwise. As Bennett grew older and engaged with other fans,
she felt the social permit to reimagine Hermione as Black or of
Mixed ethnic background, pointing to fan art that represented
this possibility: ""Racebent' characters have long been making
appearances on sites like Tumblr, but they have been picking up
heat recently. One of the most popular and frequent, at least on
my dash, was Hermione Granger as a woman of color, most often
Black. For the first time, I was seeing Hermione's subtext brought
out into text." (N.P.)

Racebending originated as part of a critique of the "whitewash-
ing" of characters of color as they entered media representations but
now also refers to fan efforts to reframe assumed white characters as
characters of color. Considering racebending as a form of fan negotiation, Henry situates her yearning for a Black Hermione in relation
to fan debates around racial representation.

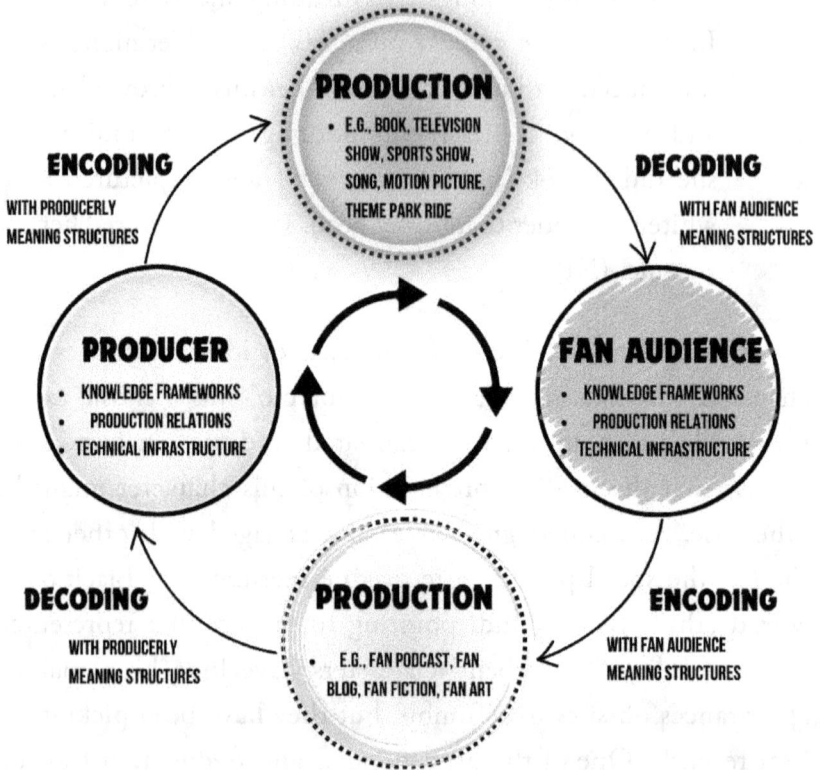

Figure 4.1: The Media Producer-Fan Audience Production Loop [original extension of Hall (1980) model].

Figure 4.1, which is titled "The Media Producer-Fan Audience Production Loop," encapsulates a dynamic interplay between media producers and fan audiences within a cyclical framework, illustrating our fandom-related extension of Hall's encoding/decoding model. In this loop, just as in Hall's original model, the process begins with producers encoding media products—such as books, sports, board games, or music albums—with culturally embedded meanings reflecting their "producerly" perspective or meaning structures. This encoding is not merely a transmission of content; it involves a complicated mixing of knowledge frameworks and production relations with the prevailing technical infrastructure, all of which shape the media's constructed messages.

As these media products (say, the *Harry Potter* books) move into the public sphere, they encounter fans (Bennett, for example) who passionately engage with these works through the decoding process. This stage is critical and aligns with Hall's theory, where audiences do not passively consume content but actively interpret and sometimes reconfigure the messages based on their own cultural and personal contexts. That negotiation may involve a mix of acceptance, adaptation, and resistance. Bennett loves the character of Hermione but also feels estranged from her, so he reimagines her as having a mixed ethnic background. In the case of our model, fans, with their passionate and collective types of engagement, may align with, reinterpret, or contest the dominant meanings proposed by the media producers. Bennett wrote that she felt firmer about her reading of Hermione as mixed race when she read what other fans wrote or appreciated the fan art she saw posted online.

Reception and Reproduction

Hall's model ends with reception and reproduction. Our media producer-fan audience loop highlights the transformational role of fans who, after decoding, participate in acts of production that then encode their own fan-related perspectives and meaning structures. This production can take place through activities like creating fantasy sports leagues, writing fan fiction, or producing podcasts, which then feed back into the original encoding process. This fan-produced content can influence subsequent media productions, suggesting a dialogic process where fan reactions and creations inform and reshape future media outputs.

Khaliah Reed (2024), one of Henry's students, noted that the characters of color in the *Harry Potter* franchise are almost all "blank slate characters," existing as names, a few defining traits or actions, and little to no interiority. These characters were added to acknowledge the presence of people of color at Hogwarts (and in the readership and fandom around the books); however, they do not give fans much to work with in terms of identification or characterization. She argues that Black fans often negotiate with these characters by rewriting them through their fan fiction, but doing so presents challenges since the source material gives them so little to work with or build upon. This is what Hall meant by reproduction—not simply the interpretation of an existing text but reimagining (and, in this case, rewriting that text) to make it fit into the audience's life world.

Reed's dissertation documents how a group of Black fans created a distinctive genre of fan fiction based on the idea of the Hogwarts Black Student Union, expanding on each other's stories and building on each other's characterizations to create a more supportive context for writing and publishing their fan works: "These stories cover a variety of subjects that range from stories inspired by the themes of Kwanzaa to what it's like to be a student at the magical school Uagadou located in continental Africa. These writers add to, deconstruct, rewrite, and reimagine the wizarding world in ways that counteract the erasure we see enacted by mainstream media and even the narrative of *Harry Potter* itself" (Reed, 2024, n.p.).

For example, several stories depict Black Hogwarts students using magic spells to deal with the problems associated with natural Black hair, suggesting that we understand these Black students as being as innovative in addressing their issues in the same way the books show White students such as Harry, Ron, and Hermione using magic to address their problems. Other stories show Black traditions of activism providing models for leadership and social change as the pupils of the school confront the dark lord Voldemort. We might see these fan writing practices as constituting particular forms of negotiation within the limits of a source text, which nevertheless has become a significant object for these fans.

Implications

Our extended model illustrates a significant shift from traditional notions of media consumption, highlighting the ongoing dialogue between producers and audiences (as occurs when Rowling adds placeholder names for diverse characters in the later books in response to her encounters with fans around the world). This feedback loop also underscores Hall's concept of "negotiated readings," where fan interactions with media are complex and varied, shaped by individual and collective interpretations that may adhere to, negotiate, or resist the encoded messages from producers. Here, the loop becomes a vivid illustration of how media is not only consumed but is continually reproduced and transformed within the cultural ecosystem.

While Hall (1980) was opening up the prospect of multiple reading positions, he also tended to ascribe a high degree of authority to the author and to the text compared to later accounts of media audiences. He describes "preferred meanings" as having "the whole social order embedded in them as a set

"Reading *Reading the Romance*"

Henry here. When I submitted my essay, "Star Trek Rerun, Reread, Rewritten" (Jenkins, 1988), to *Critical Studies in Mass Communications,* one of the peer readers assigned to the submission was Janice Radway. Though I had been rewriting the essay—one of my first academic publications--for several years, it was still a hodgepodge of theories searching for a coherent focus. Radway was a logical choice to help me whip it into shape. What I sent her was a broad case for the concept of active audiences. She felt that this battle had already been won and that what was needed at this stage in the emergence of the field was a series of more specific case studies of how particular audiences engaged with particular texts under particular circumstances.

Radway's landmark book, *Reading the Romance* (1984), was on John Fiske's seminar reading lists by the mid-1980s, so I was floored to be engaged in direct correspondence with her. In the years that followed, I came to consider her as an important missing link between audience research (as practiced by early Birmingham writers) and fandom studies (as we would define it from 1992 and beyond).

In an introduction to the second edition of *Reading the Romance,* Radway offered an explanation for how the book came to be written, insisting that she was "wholly unaware" of the sociological work of the Birmingham school on media audiences as she was writing her book. Instead, she located herself in relation to a more anthropo-logical model of literary production and consumption that was taking shape at the University of Pennsylvania under the direction of Russell Nye: "They argued that cultural investigation must always take account of spatial and temporal specificities... The department's required graduate seminars were structured around particular communities which were studied synchronically and in-depth" (p. 3-4). It was this model she passed along to me through our correspondence.

Her introduction describes how she began her project in an effort to explore whether the reading of popular literature could be conducted in a more "empirical" manner and to consider what such research might gain from more active engagement with feminist theory. She confesses, "I had not previ-ously read any romance novels" (p. 6). Radway is not a fan and was not trying to understand her own fandom, as many others in fandom studies would be. Her focus is motivated by more conventional academic concerns. She reports that her initial focus was on romance novels as literary texts, whereas it was the women in her fieldwork who taught her that what really mattered was the process of reading the romances in the context of their everyday lives: "I try to make a case for seeing romance reading as a form of individual resistance to a situation predicated on the assumption that it is women's time and privacy for women even as it addresses the corollary conse-quences of their situation, the physical exhaustion and emotional depletion

of meanings, practices, and beliefs: the everyday knowledge of social structures" (p. 136). Here, we might consider all the ways we know that Hermione is White, whether or not the books explicitly say so.

Some fan scholars leaned too heavily into the notion of fans as resistant readers in their early accounts, a position for which they were sharply criticized. Here, for example, is what Henry (Jenkins, 1992) said in *Textual Poachers*:

> From the perspective of dominant taste, fans appear to be frighten-ingly out of control, undisciplined and unre-pentant, rogue readers... Unimpressed by insti-tutional authority and expertise, the fans assert their own right to form interpretations, to offer evaluations, and to con-struct cultural canons. Undaunted by tradi-tional conceptions of literary and intellectual property, fans raid mass

culture, claiming its materials for their own use, reworking them as the basis for their own cultural creations and social interactions (p. 18).

This much-quoted passage does not directly use the term "resistant," but it is understandable why people at the time would have mapped this onto Hall's categorization. If resistance occurs, it is cultural and not political resistance to notions of appropriate interpretation and copyright restrictions. It is not resistance to consumer capitalism or neoliberalism. (We return to the notion of political resistance in **Fandom as Public** and **Fandom as Activism**).

More recently, Henry (Jenkins, 2017) has argued that fans were more apt to negotiate with preferred meanings because of the institutionalized nature of their reading practice and because surplus audiences (that is, an audience that falls outside the segmentation intended by the producer) were apt to have greater consciousness of their subordinate status than the desired audience segments might. Shannon and

brought about by the fact that no one in the patriarchal family is charged with their own care" (p. 12).

Radway embedded herself in a community of women brought together by a bookstore clerk she called "Dot," who had developed a reputation for her ability to help these readers find "good romances" that addressed their genre preferences. Throughout the book, she helps to map conventions of "good" and "bad" romances as articulated by "Dot" and the other "Smithton women." However, she also discusses reading romances as what today we might call "self-care." These women carved out time in their everyday routines to read and thus rest from their weariness, and the contents of the books gave them "hope" that other configurations of everyday life might be possible. The community of readers Radway describes served as a mutual support network, increasing the women's sense that it was okay for them to take time away from their domestic responsibilities for some pleasure of their own, much as later writers would stress the collective empowerment that fandom offered its participants.

Radway's focus was on these women as readers; my focus was on women as writers (specifically of fan fiction), but we were both taking their erotic and romantic fantasies seriously as a source of insights into shifting gender relationships in the 1980s. An understanding of reading and writing as meaningful processes in the lives of everyday women was required before fandom studies could emerge as a research paradigm.

Weaver (1948) ascribed miscommunication to noise that disrupted the signal. Fans can be noisy, for sure, but for Hall and subsequent writers, alternative readings were not the result of "misunderstandings" between viewers and authors. Rather, such ruptures occurred at the site of contestation, where alternative agendas or experiences were articulated and where the audience drew from aspects of the text that were meaningful to them.

Williams and Hall represented a first generation of people advocating for a more qualitative and ethnographic approach to audience research. John Fiske, Ian Ang, David Morley, Janice Radway, John Tulloch, and Dorothy Hobson, among others, constituted a second generation who tapped into anthropological theory and applied methodologies to develop these insights. Similarly, Elizabeth S. Bird may be a contemporary leader of ethnographic research on media audiences, alongside Ellen Seiter, Justin Lewis, Nick Couldry, and others. Bird's book, *The Audience in Everyday Life* (2003), makes a strong case (through case studies of news, politics, racial representation, etc.) for the continued value of qualitative audience research as functioning distinct from and alongside fandom studies.

In the next chapter, we will consider what audience researchers, such as John Tulloch and Martin Barker, had to say about science fiction and

Surplus Audiences

The most active fans are often "surplus audiences," unintended (or secondary and undervalued) recipients of media texts produced for other segments—female consumers of male-centered action genres, adult consumers of young adult texts, or minority consumers of mainstream media (Jenkins, Ford, and Green, 2013). These audiences are called "surplus" within the media industry because they are considered added value beyond the viewers that the industry intentionally targeted.

Such segments are desirable insofar as they create value in forms that count within the production system, such as ratings. The production's metrics do not depend upon them, but their interest may increase the return on investment. As such, these audiences need to work harder to find pleasure in these fan objects. Their interests were not consciously factored into the production decisions. However, in some cases, when the industry discovers its audiences, as well as how their views may have differed from the perspectives of fandom scholars, such as Henry, who were often writing alongside them. Later, we will watch how the conception of fandom as a global or at least transnational audience emerged from the foundational work on soap operas by Ian Ang, Elihu Katz, and Tamar Leibes.

As we conclude this chapter, our extensions and development of Hall's encoding/decoding model encourage us to reconsider the unrealized opportunities within the interdependent relationship between media producers and audiences. No longer seen as passive vessels, fan audiences are now their own producers, and these productions transpire in a media environment where they loop back into production processes to form an ongoing cycle of meaning encoding and decoding. These negotiations take place within the everyday struggles over cultural power, aligning with Williams' assertion that "culture is ordinary," and thereby, reflects the complex, intersecting identities, interests, and loyalties that audience

these unanticipated viewers, they may add elements—subplots—that reward their passion if they can do so without alienating the audience segments that advertisers and sponsors want to reach.

One common approach has been labeled "queer baiting," which Judith Fatthallah (2015) has described as a strategy for the "covert courting" of a surplus queer audience by "suggesting a queer relationship between two characters and then emphatically denying and laughing off the possibility." Initially, the goal was to reach more queer viewers who brought desired forms of expendable income without risking their core audience, which was presumed to be straight and potentially homophobic.

Consider the case of "slash" fandom, where mostly female fans of varied sexualities imagine same-sex characters having romantic and sexual feelings towards each other. As "slash" fan fiction has become better known beyond fan circles, the strategy has also been considered a viable means of attracting female fans through the use of certain genre conventions or extratextual discourses coded as "slashy." Long-term fans of *Sherlock, Supernatural, Teen Wolf,* and *Xena: Warrior Princess,* among other cult television series, have expressed profound disappointment and anger at being "strung along" through such tactics. These fans feel devalued by the way the industry sought to attract and distance them at the same time (Brennan, 2019). While producers often convince themselves that they are "teasing" fans with a fun subtext, the term "queer baiting" has become a label intended to hold the producers and brands accountable for such manipulative and exploitative practices.

Alfred Martin (2021) introduced the concept of "Surplus Blackness." In the media industry's mental model, Black audiences are always surplus, even in relation to programs with all-Black casts, which are evaluated based on whether or not they can attract a majority audience: "Black audiences are rarely explicitly courted as anything other than a value-added audience for a project (or set of projects) designed for broader, mainstream (read: white) appeal... For a blockbuster film like *Black Panther*, Black spectators were considered surplus to the target Marvel audience" (Martin, 2021, n.p.). Yet Black fans have laid claim to *Black Panther* as a vital part of their own culture, holding their own cons (Wakandacon) where the perspectives of fans of color were highlighted. A *Saturday Night Live* sketch spoofed the dynamic of "Surplus Blackness" as a group of Black fans expressed their discomfort when white audience members performed the "Wakanda Forever" salute. As one woman explained, "We know your history. You don't give stuff back."

members bring to their media interactions. Hall's work deepens our understanding of how audiences both shape and are shaped by the media they consume, revealing the tensions between dominant ideologies and the lived realities of diverse audiences.

We will now transition to the next chapter and continue our historical development of audience studies by charting its evolution into fandom studies. Where traditional audience studies focus on media consumption and meaning-making, fandom studies begin to investigate how these audiences transform into collectives full of engagement, creativity, and production. This shift reflects a growing recognition of the importance of fan culture as a site of identity formation, resistance, and collective meaning-making, offering a bridge between audience studies' formulations of acquiescent audience reception and the lively and highly engaged practices of fandom.

CHAPTER 5:

From Audience Studies to Fandom Studies

Hall's "Encoding, Decoding" model set the stage for the rapid expansion of audience research in the 1980s and 1990s, initially following Hall's own example, seeking to document the diverse audience positions and processing around the news. Gradually, it expanded into other genres, such as science fiction, where the status of the audience as fans became harder to ignore.

In this chapter, Henry will recount the tensions that surfaced in the writing of his book, *Science Fiction Audiences: Watching Star Trek and Doctor Who* (Tulloch and Jenkins, 1995), which he co-authored with John Tulloch, a founding figure in British audience research. The book's chapters represent a moment when the field of fandom studies was seeking to separate itself from the audience studies tradition that inspired it. As the chapter continues, we discuss another British audience researcher, Martin Barker, who also often wrote about audiences of horror, science fiction, and fantasy but sought to maintain a more objective social science stance in the face of the ways that fandom studies research was taking shape around influences from cultural studies and debates in anthropology. Finally, we will take up Hall's discussion of fantasy and representation in relation to race and how it might speak to contemporary writings, such as those of Ebony Thomas, regarding the Black imagination, which are informing contemporary fandom studies.

Science Fiction Audiences

Henry here. I followed *Textual Poachers* (Jenkins, 1992) with a second book, *Science Fiction Audiences: Watching Star Trek and Doctor Who* (Jenkins and Tulloch, 1994), which might be understood, retrospectively, as marking the transition from audience studies towards fandom studies. John Tulloch, my co-author, was a long-time audience researcher who would later write an important overview of audience research, *Watching Television Audiences* (Tulloch, 2000). Throughout our book, Tulloch primarily refers to "audiences," while I discuss "fans," a distinction neither of us noted at the time. The case studies Tulloch wrote drew on several decades of sociological research into the ways different groups of people responded to the long-running British television show *Doctor Who*, groups selected less on the basis of fan engagement than demographic categories, many of them university students who have historically been the most accessible communities for social science research. Although it was a niche public television show in the U.S., supported in the 1990s by a core fan audience that was expanding rapidly, *Doctor Who* was an institution in the United Kingdom (UK). Almost every British kid watched the Doctor's adventures in time and space as they were growing up, and many continued to watch into their college and young adult years. At the time, my wife and son were passionate fans of *Doctor Who*, having gone back to watch all of the Doctors while I was an interested viewer of only the most recent episodes. I brought my lifelong fandom of *Star Trek* to the project.

Tulloch had originally conducted this research with the anticipation it would be included in *Doctor Who: The Unfolding Text* (Tulloch and Alvarado, 1983), but it was cut for length reasons from the book, which already included lengthy production histories and close textual analysis. As he notes in *Science Fiction Audiences*:

> The early part of the audience research took place immediately prior to, and concurrently with, the circulation of David Morley's *Nationwide Audience* book, and reflected similar preoccupations: the concern with the excessive textual formalism of 1970s *Screen* theory and a wish to deal with 'actual' audiences; the emphasis on political and ideological readings of popular television; the focus on audience's 'meaning systems' as a function of their positioning in relation to society's 'dominant' values… the *Doctor Who* project chose groups of sociology students and mechanical engineers to discuss a text focusing on social changes as a result of breakthroughs in engineering technology. In Morley's case, and mine, the audience research was premised on the notion of decoding as an ideological process" (Jenkins and Tulloch, 1995, p. 66).

Tulloch notes another important difference: David Morely's *Nationwide Audiences* (1980), which Tulloch references above, had tested Hall's encoding/decoding model through focus groups of viewers of a British news program constituted for the research. Tulloch sought people who were already committed viewers of *Doctor Who* and thus could be expected to be familiar with its genre conventions.

I took this approach a step further, focusing on fan communities and working with collaborators who were deeply embedded in those communities. For example, for my study of the Gaylaxians, a group of LGBTQ (or "queer") fans, I worked with John Campbell, a remarkably bright young man who I met at a fan gathering and who showed great curiosity for the work. Campbell (2004) became so infatuated with this research that he went to graduate school, got his doctorate, and became a significant researcher exploring gay men's online communities.

John Fiske had introduced me to Tulloch, who was seeking a collaborator who might refresh and add to these case studies of science fiction audiences. Beginning while I was finishing *Textual Poachers*, my cases had been conducted more recently and were shaped by the goal of showing how different groups of fans drawn to *Star Trek* might prioritize different aspects of the series and adopt different reading strategies. For example, as a new faculty member at Massachusetts Institute of Technology (MIT) , I was fascinated with how my students thought and how many of them had been drawn to their fields through the realm of science fiction stories. I asked one of my undergraduate students, Greg Dancer, to interview some of his contemporaries in their dorm rooms with a tape recorder in hand. Then, I wrote an analysis to help contextualize what he found.

Tulloch was interested in how audiences were positioned in relation to different discourses of science fiction, discourses that emerged from different subgenres but also different ideologies. On the one hand, there was what he described as "institutional rationalism" and "scientism," which he linked to both gender and class positions, i.e., male university students. In contrast, he was also interested in the "utopianism" associated with feminist responses to the genre. Tulloch explored Hall's moment of reception and interpretation. I was more—but not exclusively—interested in the ways these texts were reproduced. MIT students deployed *Star Trek* in discussions of scientific and engineering problem-solving. Female fans saw the franchise as a springboard for writing fanfiction about gender relations. The Gaylaxians used the series for inspiration, imagining alternatives to a homophobic society. I also noted an interesting distinction: the MIT students tended to focus on the characters as autonomous problem solvers, identifying when each "saved the ship." The Gaylaxians, and especially the fanzine writers, tended to read the characters in relation to each other—as friends, mentors, and lovers.

These tensions remained unresolved because Tulloch and I wrote the whole book without ever meeting each other face-to-face and without ever interacting in real-time. At a time when networked communications were still emerging, we corresponded through the mail or through fax rather than email, each writing their own sections and editing them together to form a book with only a few passages co-authored. When I finally met Tulloch, I realized that I could not have written the book any other way since he was a formal (some might say "stuffy") British academic several decades older than me. I found him more than a little intimidating. Yet, at a distance, I felt free to revise and rewrite a significant amount of his prose to make it livelier and more readable.

When Tulloch (2000) wrote about fans, he did so as if they constituted a special audience, which he saw as a "powerless elite." Fans, he argued, were "elite" in that they were highly knowledgeable about *Doctor Who*, had formed sophisticated opinions about what constituted "golden ages" or "unforgivable" failures in the history of the show, and had built institutions, such as fan conventions and zines, with their own established ways of doing things and ways of thinking. They had inside knowledge of the production process and felt sufficient ownership over the text to be ready to argue with the producers about the directions they had chosen for the series. They were "powerless" in that, despite such commitment and knowledge, they had little to no direct influence over their fan object. Indeed, producers often argue that they have to break with fan opinion because fans, as an elite or exception, are not representative of the general public, the primary audience necessary to reach critical mass.

I was arguing to the contrary that fans were not "powerless," even if they lacked the power of those involved in the production process. They saw themselves as empowered, as I demonstrated when I traced the activities of the Gaylaxians to get a queer character added to *Star Trek: The Next Generation*. These fan-activists had been able to extract a promise from Gene Roddenberry and sought to hold subsequent producers accountable for that commitment, even in the face of repeated efforts to explain away the problem of sexual representation or to deflect the issue into allegories and metaphors rather than direct representation. In short, these fans had some power, but not enough to ultimately determine the outcome of their protests without cooperation from producers. On the other hand, their efforts have now resulted in the inclusion of multiple queer and trans characters, such as Dr Hugh Culber and Paul Stammets on *Star Trek: Discovery*.

An Early Critic of Fandom Studies

Henry here. Martin Barker was another British audience studies researcher who, like Tulloch, wrote about genre works that had strong fan followings, who often drew his 'audiences' from fan communities but who never felt comfortable in fandom studies (Hills, 2023). Instead, Barker chose to embrace the sociological models of reception, inspired by Hall's encoding/decoding model while doing ambitious projects mapping the global reception of the television adaptation of George R. R. Martin's *Game of Thrones* (Barker, Smith, and Atwood, 2023) or Peter Jackson's *The Lord of the Rings* trilogy (Barker 2006).

Hills (2023) describes Barker as a "rogue" in relation to fandom studies in part because he refused to take a stable position in regard to the value of fandom, unlike early fandom studies figures like myself who were critiquing the pathologization of fandom. He also rejects the field's focus on self-positioning, which gets shorthanded as the "aca-fan" turn. As Hills writes,

For Barker, his own positioning was a distraction—what he wanted was to gather an empirically convincing portrait of what audiences, fans among them, were doing with texts. In this regard, his personal media consumption was largely treated as an irrelevance rather than a vital concern, as it would arguably become for fan studies. (pp. 30-31)

My contributions to *Science Fiction Audiences* were experimenting with a more proximate and subjective mode of writing about media audiences. I accepted that fandom constituted a particular kind of culture, which I understood from the inside as a participant observer rather than from the outside as "objective social scientists" who often constructed the audiences they were studying in a laboratory setting.

According to Hills, Barker and others objected to the lack of attention to methodology in our writing, suggesting that it constituted a new form of journalism. Indeed, my own work was consciously informed by my reading of the new journalists, such as Tom Wolfe, Truman Capote, or Hunter S. Thompson, who experimented with novelistic modes of writing to convey how their subjects thought and felt. This approach included writing a critical analysis of the fan objects as if from the point of view of the fandoms I studied, a practice especially pervasive in my essay, "Out of the Closet and Into the Universe," in *Science Fiction Audiences* (Tulloch and Jenkins, 1994). My writing for the book was also informed by my reading of Renato Rosaldo's *Culture and Truth* (1993), which made the case for new modes of ethnographic writing that acknowledged the process of the anthropologist's encounter with another culture rather than claiming to exist outside the culture, which they neither touched nor were touched by.

Inspired by the ca-fan stance, the emerging group of fandom scholars was seeking to explore how we knew what we knew about fandom. We were seeking to construct our pictures of particular fandom communities on the basis of an eclectic mix of materials—bits of fan writing in zines or discussion lists, interviews to clarify our understanding of their interpretive logic and descriptions of our own experiences as fans or guests of fan communities.

In keeping with the social science tradition, the audience researchers wrote in a neutral or transparent style; fandom studies writers were beginning to adopt a more self-conscious style that deployed the insider jokes and slang of the fan communities they were studying. This style was one of the many ways we sought to signal our own stakes in the topics we were researching. The debates distinguishing fandom studies and audience studies replicated in a microcosm the debates separating old and new modes of humanistic writing; fandom studies generally embraced a more avant-garde approach that valued transparency about our relations to our objects of study rather than making claims to objectivity that were breaking down all around us.

Science Fiction Audiences includes some of my most experimental writing, perhaps in response to the more social science mode that Tulloch brought to the project. I recall struggling with Tulloch and with my publisher over my use of the first-person. Yet, there seemed to be no other way to write about marching in the Boston Gay Pride Parade with the Gaylaxians, for example—a personally meaningful act at a time when I was coming out as bisexual. For that matter, I also needed first person to convey an understanding of how MIT students read *Star Trek: The Next Generation*, which had emerged from my own classroom experiences teaching science fiction.

Barker had been a mentor for Hills and many others in British fan studies, helping to explain why they deviated in some important ways from the American fandom studies tradition. The British researchers were characterized by a greater focus on individual fans rather than fan communities and a greater reliance on social science models (note the reference to the field as "fan studies" rather than "fandom studies," signaling this more individualized focus). Like Barker, Hills has built his career around very close, sometimes painfully close, readings of the particular language and often implicit argumentative structures of other writers, myself included, deconstructing their implicit logic and looking for points of tension and contradiction.

Hills (2023) writes,

> While he generally maintained a critical distance from fan studies,... Barker's work can, in fact, be argued to represent one of the strongest realizations of the ethical underpinnings of first wave fan studies, not due to a celebratory 'fandom is beautiful' valorization, but rather via a principled dismantling of the politics of Othering through which comic book, horror, fantasy and porn fandoms were all variously—and highly problematically—figured as deviant audiences needing to be governmentally/discursively policed. In relation to fans, rather than fan studies, Barker was dedicated to undermining discourses that denigrated pop culture fandoms (p. 31).

Hills suggest that Barker positioned himself as an in-house critic of the emerging field of fandom studies, seeking to hold onto what he saw as most valuable in the earlier audience studies research. He questioned the persistence of representations of fans as resistant audiences and the failure to explore the boundary policing of fan communities as well as to look more closely at reactionary dimensions of fan discourse. Much as he was critical of "moral panics" that mischaracterized fans and popular texts, he also questioned the figure of the fan and of the researcher that was then emerging within cultural studies. Hills (2023) summarizes

Barker's conception of the fan as follows: "The testable definition of fandom is that it features an unusual viewing strategy—a way of relating to a fan object—which actively denies and counters any experienceable 'moment of closure,' and hence always allows for the possibility of new discussion, analysis, understanding and experience of the fan object" (p. 41). Hills argues that Barker anticipated more recent developments in fan and fandom studies in many significant ways.

Barker's focus on dismantling discourses that positioned fandoms as deviant audiences aligns with contemporary efforts to destigmatize fan practices and explore their broader cultural legitimacy. For example, his interrogation of moral panics parallels current studies that examine the politics of representation within fandoms, such as the debate over diversity in media and the backlash it often provokes in certain fan communities. Moreover, Barker's rejection of simplistic portrayals of fans as purely resistant audiences anticipated nuanced understandings of fan ambivalence and the complex power dynamics within fan communities. His emphasis on boundary policing within fandoms has influenced analyses of exclusionary practices such as gatekeeping and toxicity in online fan cultures. This perspective aligns with recent work examining reactionary and conservative dimensions of fandom, including the resurgence of exclusionary ideologies within certain subcultures. Finally, Barker's conception of fandom as an ongoing and open-ended interpretive practice also presaged scholarly attention to participatory and co-creative aspects of fandom. Studies on transformative works and grassroots activism echo Barker's framing of fandom as a space of continual dialogue, reinterpretation, and innovation. These connections reveal how Barker's critical distance from fandom studies allowed him to illuminate foundational dynamics that remain central to the field's evolution right up to the present day.

Representation, Fantasy, and Pleasure

Both here. In the essay "What is This 'Black' in Black Popular Culture?" Stuart Hall (1992b) focuses on the implications of his encoding/decoding model for understanding how race operates in contemporary culture. While acknowledging the "contradictory" and often "deformed, incorporated, and unauthentic" forms popular culture takes in its representations of Black identity, Hall also sees something there worth negotiating with: "Black popular culture has enabled the surfacing, inside the mixed and contradictory modes even of some mainstream popular culture, of elements of a discourse that is different—other forms of life, other traditions of representation" (Hall, 1992b, p. 470).

Representation matters, Hall (1992b) tells us, because it shapes the language through which people understand their own lives and through which others understand who they are—not because popular culture offers a realistic representation of lived experience but because popular culture is "profoundly mythic... a theater of popular desires, a theater of popular fantasies... where we discover and play with the identifications of ourselves, where we are imagined, where we are represented, not only to the audiences out there who do not get the message but to ourselves for the first time" (p. 474).

Intervention Analysis

Henry here. I framed "Out of the Closet and Into the Universe" as what John Hartley (1992) had called "intervention analysis." Hartley co-wrote a book, *Reading Television,* with John Fiske (Fiske and Hartley, 1978) and maintained a close friendship with my mentor; the two developed a rich intellectual conversation early in my career, which persists to the present day.

Hartley (1992) wrote: "Intervention analysis seeks not only to describe and explain existing dispositions of knowledge, but also to change them... Intervention analysis certainly needs to take popular television more or less as it finds it, without high-culture fastidiousness or right on political squeamishness, but it needs to intervene *in* the media and in the production of popular knowledge about it" (pp. 5-7). Intervention, here, refers to a critical posture that combines critique and advocacy, which uses the status of the academy to amplify and promote popular efforts by

Tulloch's "powerless elite" to advocate change in the content or structures of media.

We might see the roots of Hartley's intervention analysis in the work of Dorothy Hobson (1982), a key figure in the emergence of audience research who helped to advocate on behalf of soap opera fans but who has generally not been discussed in relation to the roots of fandom studies. Hobson wrote *Crossroads: The Drama of a Soap Opera* about a long-running British soap opera that had become an institution in the lives of its fans, whom she identifies as older women, especially "pensioners," who identify with many of the characters. Her goal had been to look at both the encoding and decoding processes around this show, chosen because it was not exceptional but everyday, or, to use one of Raymond Williams' terms, "ordinary." However, it was also very meaningful to the people who watched it.

The book begins with the story of the firing of Noele Gordon, who had been a staple of *Crossroads* for decades. She takes us inside the studio to understand the rationale for the sacking, which had been the focus of numerous news stories but not a sustained analysis. As the book progresses, though, Hobson becomes more and more emphatic about the concerns of the audience, helping us to understand what the firing of this beloved actress means from their point of view. She traces how the producers sought to build a sense of ownership amongst this audience for a series they did not themselves respect.

This focus on fantasy and myth makes Hall's discussion valuable for understanding fandom. Fantasies about magic or superpowers are ultimately myths about power—who possesses it, who is entitled to it, who deploys it, toward what ends, and on whose behalf. Struggles over how race operates in fantastical genres are essential when we consider how important these stories are for younger readers, who are in the process of mapping their place in the social order. It matters, say, that Orcs and Klingons are depicted as Black in *The Lord of The Ring* trilogy and the *Star Trek* universe, respectively, while Tolkien's Wizards, Elves, and Hobbits are depicted as White, since the latter are most often the heroes of the narratives.

Ebony Elizabeth Thomas, in her book *The Dark Fantastic* (2019), warns about the "imagination gap," where white children are much more often represented and encouraged to read works of fantasy that enable heroic identifications and thus feed an assumption of white empowerment. Black children are given a steady diet of realistic fictions that deal with social problems, often in pessimistic ways, and thus leave them feeling defeated and overwhelmed. She stresses the importance of encouraging all children to "dream" of alternative worlds. However, she also notes that children do not always read what they are told and shares her own experiences as a young Black girl who was a fan of the very white Canadian stories about *Anne of Green Gables*, introducing her to a world far beyond her own urban American experiences.

People of color have historically been excluded from representation within the speculative genres (such as science fiction and fantasy). Still, new, imperfect, problematic representations are starting to emerge amid often white backlash about the unfamiliar presence of Black mermaids and stormtroopers (Proctor, 2020). As fans of color work through their responses to these shifts, dealing with differing degrees of inclusion, marginalization, exoticization, and misrepresentation, and yet also pleasure, recognition, and empowerment, Hall's work provides us with a core foundation for our analysis.

She describes the helplessness the audience felt when the character they liked best was taken away from them.

She discusses the way the *Crossroads* audience experienced the removal of this character—another indignity they felt was imposed on them because the producers did not respect and value them as viewers. The production professionals feared that the popular but critically dismissed series would not help them advance their careers because it was not a show that others in the industry watched and valued. Hobson writes about the protest letters sent to the network and newspapers about the decision:

> If this book has an overwhelming aim, it is to argue for the importance of the television audience and the need for that perspective to be considered in relation to the programmes they wish to watch. The letters which I read contained such overwhelming evidence of their involvement with *Crossroads* that it would be difficult not to recognize what the programme meant to them. I make no apology for the mixture of emotions and analysis which pervades this chapter for it is necessary if it is to reflect the tone of the letters and present a picture of sections of the audience about whom we know very little. (p. 138)

At the time, Hobson was attacked for her naivety in seeking to shift the industry to pay more attention to this audience and for not showing sufficient academic objectivity in how she characterized their response. Again, it is striking that Hobson does not frame these committed and impassioned audiences as "fans" in the way we are using the concept across **Frames of Fandom**. She still sees them as individual viewers, not as part of a larger fandom, and thus tells us little to nothing about how they organized a letter-writing campaign to speak back to the decision-makers who affected *Crossroads*. Today, much of what she says may seem a bit obvious, a starting point for dealing with controversies between producers and fans. She was just asking that the voices of these older female viewers be heard and respected.

Inspired by Hartley and Hobson, my chapter, "Out of the Closet and Into the Universe" in *Science Fiction Audiences* (Tulloch and Jenkins, 1995), sought to understand why queer fans were particularly drawn to *Star Trek* for exploring possible futures where they might be included within the diversity of races and species onboard the Starship Enterprise. I wanted to understand why the producers continued to defer a commitment Gene Roddenberry, the creator of the series, had made before he died to make a queer character appear in the series. At places, I articulated the voice of the series fans in response to frustrating and disappointing statements—excuses, really—for why it would be "inappropriate" to incorporate queer characters into the series. Like the fans with whom I spoke, I resented the ways that producers sought to use allegorical episodes to speak to the "issue" of queerness rather

As we conclude this chapter on the evolution from audience studies to fandom studies, we must remind ourselves that fandom, as a subject of research, began to take shape in opposition to the more detached methodologies of traditional audience studies. Although scholars like John Tulloch and Martin Barker maintained a sociological distance in their analysis of genre audiences, early fandom studies embraced a more engaged and immersive approach to the topic, recognizing the extent to which the unique interpretive practices and community dynamics differentiate fandoms from general audiences. These foundational tensions within the field laid the groundwork for more nuanced understandings of media consumption. Hall's encoding/decoding model provided a crucial starting point. However, as the field progressed, scholars of fandom developed new ideas to account for the deeply personal, creative, and often transgressive modes of fan engagement they were finding, particularly around genre shows like *Star Trek* and *Doctor Who*. At that point, when fandom was recognized not simply as a special type of audience but as a distinct cultural practice, audience studies had branched off into the field of fandom studies.

This shift toward fandom studies reflects broader changes in the global media landscape, where the circulation of media texts across national and cultural borders has become a central area of inquiry. Our next chapter will explore how global networks and audience reception processes further complicate the relationship between fans, media texts, and producers. Just as the television show *Dallas* sparked debates around American cultural imperialism and Bollywood fostered cross-cultural engagement in Africa, these examples underscore the

than including queer characters within the utopian vision of the future these fans had come to accept as Roddenberry's worldview.

The fans could write their own stories—and they did—which portrayed one or another of the series regulars as queer; however, they were concerned about a situation that could not be addressed in subtext. Many fans told me that they cared about this issue of representation because they were concerned about the number of youth in the LGBTQ community who were committing suicide because they felt alone in the world and saw no future for themselves. They wanted a reassuring statement that would be made if such characters were openly acknowledged as a normal part of a series with a long history of pushing for diversity and inclusion. I focused on this conflict because I felt it would elucidate how audiences read science fiction through a history of feminist and queer interventions. I also sought to use Hartley's intervention analysis to amplify their voices.

importance of understanding how fan communities form and function within diverse cultural contexts. The transnational case studies in the next chapter will enable us to explore how global audiences negotiate meaning across different cultural frameworks, illustrating how media texts travel, transform, and take on new meanings as they pass through complex networks of interpretation and engagement.

CHAPTER 6:

From *Dallas* to Bollywood: The Globalization of Audience Research

The emergence of fan audiences as a subject of serious academic inquiry has allowed researchers to explore how media circulates across different cultural contexts and the active role that audiences play in interpreting, negotiating, and transforming what they consume. We will return to these issues in **Fandom as an Agent of Globalization**. This chapter explores several key studies that investigate fan reception on a global scale, examining the cultural particulars of media consumption among audiences throughout diverse geographies, including Europe, Israel, and Nigeria.

The scholars explored in this chapter, such as Ien Ang, Tamar Liebes, Elihu Katz, and Brian Larken, each developed unique methodologies to understand transnational consumption, raising critical questions about cultural imperialism, negotiation, and audience interpretation. Ang's work, for example, demonstrates that audiences' pleasures and frustrations with *Dallas* offer insights into how cultural meaning is constructed in different contexts, while Liebes and Katz provide a more structured approach to understanding how cultural codes shape interpretations of media texts across ethnically diverse Israeli communities. These inquiries into different national audiences highlight the ways in which local values and social norms influence their reception of the program. Through our engagement with these foundational studies, this chapter sets the stage for further discussions of how fan audiences function, both in relation to Western media products and their own cultural contexts, opening a path for considering how these dynamics play out in the complex transculturality of contemporary media environments, as seen in the example of Larken's work on Bollywood fandom in Nigeria.

Watching *Dallas*

In the late 1980s and early 1990s, the American prime-time melodrama *Dallas* was the most popular television series in the world, having found success in more than 90 countries, with Brazil (with its own local production of telenovelas) and Japan as notable exceptions. *Dallas* also became central to debates in many of these countries about America's cultural influence, often described in terms of models of cultural imperialism. Audience studies researchers such as Ien Ang in the Netherlands and Tamar Liebes and Elihu Katz in Israel set out to test this framing by engaging directly with the audiences of the series.

Ang solicited letters from people who have "strong feelings" about *Dallas,* both positive and negative, to understand the "pleasures" and emotions this melodramatic text generated. Her introduction to *Watching Dallas* (Ang, 1985) identifies Ang's core focus:

> Nobody is forced to watch television; at most, people can be led to it by effective advertising. What, then, are the determining factors of this enjoyment, this pleasure?... In order to answer such questions, we should not inquire

about the social, economic, and psychological characteristics of the public, but should rather ask ourselves what
happens in the process of watching *Dallas*. It is in the
actual confrontation between viewer and programme that
pleasure is primarily generated (Ang, 1985, pp. 10-11).

Ang based the book's analysis on 42 letters from people who
"love" or "hate" the series, responding to an advertisement she took
out soliciting reactions. The problem at the time was how to gather
sufficient evidence of audience responses. This issue flipped with
the emergence of the internet as a place where fan discussions could
take place, with any given online discussion list generating hundreds
of responses per day and some discussions constituting thousands
of posts over months of conversation amongst large groups of participants. The problem we have now is how to sort through such
plenitude and how to set priorities about what examples to center
on in our analysis. However, Ang was working during a much earlier
time, and her respondents were almost entirely European (mostly
Dutch)—a starting point, certainly, for understanding the cross-cultural reception of a globally transmitted series.

Ang's analysis discovered that those who disliked the television
show *Dallas* found it easier to explain and justify their perspectives
than those who liked, even loved, the series:

> "We have seen that the letter-writers who like *Dallas* have
> difficulty in stating why they do. Many of them finally
> have to admit that they don't know. This uncertainty is
> not surprising, as the experience of pleasure is not ratio-
> nally motivated... Pleasure is one of the things in life
> regarded as self-evident and which, as a rule, people don't
> think about" (Ang, 1985, p. 86).

Note the somewhat clunky formulation, "letter-writers who like *Dallas*" rather than fans. We do not know which of these respondents participated in a larger fandom, but they are, by our definition, fans. Ang understands them as members of an audience. In the passage above, Ang falls back on the notion of the fan as inarticulate, which much of the early fandom studies literature questioned. Fans in fandom studies research had much to say about why and how they took pleasure in their fan objects.

On the other hand, Ang anticipated the study of anti-fandom as a rich site for understanding how meaning-making takes place around popular television (see more below). Those who disliked *Dallas* had ready access to critical discourses against mass culture that instructed what arguments could be made. Here, she found evidence of distaste among Europeans for American influence on their local culture and a kind of folk theory of cultural imperialism. She also found evidence of an anti-fan response shaped by anti-capitalism and feminist discourse, which was also widely accessible to her Dutch respondents.

She concludes:

> The ideology of mass culture therefore not only offers a (negative) label for the programme itself, but also serves as a mould for the way in which a large number of haters of *Dallas* account for their displeasure....' And so the ideology of mass culture fulfills a comforting and reassuring role: it makes a search for more detailed and personal explanations superfluous, because it provides a finished explanatory model that convinces, sounds logical and radiates legitimacy (pp. 95–96).

Those letter writers who hated *Dallas* did so because they despised mass culture, a stance widely embraced as sophisticated within their European context.

Israel's Diverse Audiences

Tamar Liebes and Elihu Katz (1990) sought to understand "How in the world is a program like *Dallas* so universally understandable, or is it? Is it understood the same way in different places? Does it evoke different kinds of involvement and response?" (Liebes and Katz, 1990, p. 3) To answer these questions, they made a series of research design decisions consistent with the more social science research practices associated with audience research, decisions that stress objectivity over positionality:

> We assembled small groups of family and friends, each group consisting of three married couples of like age, education, and ethnicity. Forty-Four such groups were chosen from among Israeli Arabs, newly arrived Russian Jews, veteran Moroccan settlers, and members of the kibbutzim (typically second-generation Israelis). Each group met in the home of one of the couples on the Saturday night of the *Dallas* broadcast, together with a trained interviewer who, following the broadcast, led a discussion based on a standardized set of guidelines (p. 6).

They further tested their findings with sample interviews with America-based viewers to see how *Dallas* was interpreted in its country of origin, as well as in Japan, to see how it was received in a country where it had failed to gain traction. Henry and his contemporaries in fandom studies felt impatient with this "arm's length" relationship with media audiences, wanting to engage more collaboratively and spontaneously with the fandoms they were researching and seeking new methodologies with which to do so. They embraced a process of participant observation that went beyond the structured focus group interviews. They considered their own approach to be closer to the ethnographic approaches deployed by contemporary anthropologists.

Liebes and Katz framed their study explicitly in relation to Hall's Encoding/Decoding model: "Whatever the message in the text—if there is one—our interest is in what message reaches the viewers. We argue that ideology is not produced through a process of stimulus and response but rather through a process of negotiation between various types of senders and receivers" (p. 4). Their findings dug deep into what Hall had described as "social codes," which shaped how audiences understood what they were watching, including, in this case, the different models of family relations that these variously culturally located viewers were applying to their comprehension of the conflicts amongst family members that constituted much of the plot of *Dallas*. They found, for example, that Russians read the *Dallas* episodes ideologically, while the Americans read them within a psychological or often psychoanalytic framework. From the perspective of what fandom studies would become, they do so based on interpretations of one discussion session rather than from the larger cultural context the ongoing activities of a fandom provide.

While they seemed uninterested in whether their interview subjects regarded themselves as fans of *Dallas*, they were interested in the process of collaborative interpretation, the "mutual aid in decoding" they observed in their focus groups. They recognized that media consumption was frequently social rather than taking place in the head of an autonomous viewer:

> Each consensus that arises from the process of mutual aid—whether of legitimation, orientation, interpretation, or the several forms of evaluation—takes on a new life as a conversational resource. The group makes use of these shared concepts and values. The group adopts

into its culture the array of words, characters, metaphors, ideas and attitudes which were verbalized as mutual aid and uses them as a symbolic vocabulary to enter even deeper into relevant issues and problems (pp. 91-92).

Knowingly or not, Katz and Leibes described what fans got out of their experience of active participation within fandom, the ways that reading a text together helps to shape their interpretive protocols, and certain kinds of conversations take place.

Bollywood in Nigeria

Let's consider a third and final example of a project that seeks to understand the audience for popular media texts that circulate beyond the culture that produced them—Brian Larkin's 1997 article, "Indian Films and Nigerian Lovers," which concerns the popularity of Bollywood movies amongst Nigerian media audiences. The first thing we need to note is that Larkin's frame of reference is anthropology and not sociology, already marking an important distinction from the earlier waves of audience research. Second, his focus is not on the circulation of an American text like *Dallas* to Europe or Israel but rather on the circulation and cross-cultural consumption of media within the global south.

His goal is a more nuanced account of how media circulates and how cultural impulses from elsewhere are absorbed or transformed as the media texts are consumed in the receiving country. Larkin's essay begins,

The sight of a 15 ft image of Sridevi, dancing erotically on the screens of the open-air cinemas of northern Nigeria, or the tall, angular figure of Amitabh Bachchan radiating charisma through the snowy, crackly reception of domestic television have become powerful, resonant images in Hausa popular culture. To this day, stickers of Indian films and stars decorate the taxis and buses of the north, posters of Indian films adorn the walls of tailors' shops and mechanics' garages, and love songs from Indian film songs are borrowed by religious singers who change the words to sing praises to the Prophet Mohammed. For over thirty years, Indian films, their stars and fashions, music and stories have been a dominant part of everyday popular culture in northern Nigeria (p. 406).

Larkin's writing is grounded not in a cluster of focus groups but from a more expansive ethnographic experience that allows him to paint a vivid picture of the dynamic status of these films in one of the multiple cultures that constitute contemporary Nigeria. Watching such films, he argues that they offer "Hausa viewers a way of imaginatively engaging with forms of tradition different from their own at the same time as conceiving of a modernity that comes without the political and ideological significance of that of the West" (Larkin, 1997, p. 407). He is interested in the "imaginative investment" viewers make in these films and the ways they deploy them to think through their own identities as members of a culture seeking models of modernity not beholden to the West.

His research takes him beyond the initial moment of reception to the ways that the Hausa youth created new works—not precisely fan fiction but related to it—which shows how they are building on these outside influences to create something new. He considers these new texts as a means of working through changing ideologies of love and family within a culture undergoing profound transitions and transformations. While he discusses people who love these films and consume them in meaningful and creative ways, Larkin does not refer to them as fans, seeing the consumption of Indian movies in Nigeria as normative and mainstream rather than as occurring within a community constituted around shared interests. Nevertheless, his focus on the creativity of media audiences aligns well with the concerns of fandom studies, and his work has been embraced as a model for studying fandom in the Global South.

The case studies of *Dallas* in the Netherlands and Israel, as well as Bollywood in Nigeria, illustrate not only the dynamic nature of fan audiences but also the presence of global networks that facilitate the movement of media across cultural and geographic boundaries. This chapter should impress upon us that fandom and audience engagement are inherently networked phenomena, with media texts traveling through complex webs of distribution, reception, and reinterpretation. Whether through transnational television markets or informal exchanges of media via diaspora communities, these networks enable media content to be appropriated and recontextualized. When it was originally aired, *Dallas* reached millions of viewers worldwide, not as a static American export but as a piece of popular culture: mass culture becoming interpreted through the specific social and cultural lenses of its global audiences. Similarly, Bollywood's influence in Nigeria highlights how media texts can move across non-Western networks, where viewers creatively engage with foreign media to negotiate their own modernities. Both cases demonstrate the centrality of networks—both formal and informal—in fashioning the transnational flows of media and its local reworkings.

As we transition into the next chapter, "Networks and Audiences," we want to emphasize the centrality of these global networks. These networks are not just channels of distribution but also spaces for audience activity and collective interpretation. In the current media landscape, networks facilitate rapid, theoretically borderless interactions among audience members, enabling them to share ideas, construct new meanings, and expand their engagement with media texts in ways that transcend the traditional modalities of audience behavior. By examining how networked communication technologies have transformed these audience relationships, we can better comprehend how the global exchange of media—and the fandom it fosters—operates in an era of digital hyperconnectivity.

CHAPTER 7:
Networks and Audiences

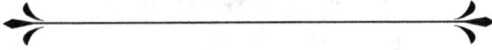

The emergence of networked communication has meant that more and more people consume popular culture online and in dialogue with others. When fan theories are proposed, memes or fan fiction are circulated, or fan videos are created, people do so with the anticipation that there is an audience out there who shares their passions and wants to see what they have produced. Reading a television show within a social network enhances our capacity to deal with narrative complexities, as we have developed a dependence on online resources to help us decode ever more complex texts.

When we refer to social networks, we are not exclusively referring to the digital realm. People engaged with media through social networks before the availability of social media. For example, Richard Dyer (1986) sought to understand the meanings gay fans attached to the performer Judy Garland in the pre-Stonewall era when the majority of gay fans were still in the closet. A shared set of meanings and associations clustered around the performer, who ultimately acknowledged a close and intimate relationship with these fans through informal conversations and newsletters that addressed matters of concern to this community. This sense of ownership and connection took shape over time through many social interactions and became such a firm part of queer culture in America in the 1950s and 1960s that it was literally worth fighting for. The Stonewall Riot, considered to be the turning point in the American Gay Rights movement, erupted when police raided a gay bar, the Stonewall Inn, in New York City on the night fans were holding a wake for the deceased singer. The rainbow flag, which is emblematic of this movement, is meant as a homage to the song "Somewhere Over the Rainbow," which Garland sings in *The Wizard of Oz.*

Forensic Fandom

Jason Mittell (2016) describes the activities within a fan network as "forensic fandom… [which] invites viewers to dig deeper, probing beneath the surface to understand the complexity of a story and its telling. Such programs create magnets for engagement, drawing viewers into story worlds and urging them to drill down to discover more" (n.p.). He suggests that, increasingly, producers anticipate and build space for fan networks to process complex information or resolve gaps that surface in the window between the aired episodes. Jenkins (1995) discusses the fans of the cult television show *Twin Peaks* in terms of their roles as problem-solvers who sought to decode a text that made them feel superior because it was considered more demanding than the average television series of the era. He observes something interesting: television critics complained that David Lynch and Mark Frost's series was becoming so complicated that it lost many viewers, whereas the fans on the internet discussion list complained that it was too easy to anticipate developments and that *Twin Peaks* was no longer challenging. He notes the difference in the level of complexity required to entertain a single viewer in their living room or to engage a networked audience working through plot developments together in a discussion forum.

Mittell's initial example of forensic fandom is the Lostpedia, a fan-created online wiki dedicated to the TV show *Lost*, where fans pooled knowledge to deal with the various mysteries surrounding the show's crash survivors and the island. Still, he has since extended the concept to consider the collective problem-solving strategies fans deployed in processing the popular podcast *Serial*. As he explains, "Highly serialized genres such as soap operas have always bred fan archivists and textual experts, while sports fans have a long history of drilling down statistically and collecting artifacts to engage more deeply with a team or player" (Mittell, 2016, n.p.).

Henry (Jenkins, 2006) uses Pierre Levy's notion of "collective intelligence" (Levy, 1999) to discuss the workings of *Survivor* fans as they seek to "spoil" the program, trying to track down information about who the contestants are, what the location is, and who got booted off first before this information was revealed in the series. He demonstrates the sophisticated ways that people pooled information or tracked down data as they sought to solve real-world mysteries. Levy considers collective intelligence within a network society as a new source of power that is as profound in its own way as the acts of colonization and corporatization that empowered earlier interests. For Levy, this new source of power is more democratic because it is more dispersed and, in its ideal form, diverse, since these traits allow the network to source and process a wider array of information.

Whether within a single family, the closed community of gay bars, or an expansive online network, fans process information, share feelings, make meaning, and debate interpretations together. We see that being social as a key element of being a fan is one of the traits that separates fandom from a more generic definition of an audience.

Generational Fandoms

Taste is never simply a matter of individual preference. What we like is shaped, often profoundly, by other people's influence in our lives. More often than not, media consumption is a shared practice—we take a date to the movies, we watch television shows with our family, we play video games with our friends, and we talk about all of it at the office the next day. Fandom takes these interactions to the next step, making social exchanges around media content a central element of our social lives. We form social relations with other people because they share our tastes.

This phenomenon is closely tied to the concept of homophily, the tendency for individuals to form connections with those who are similar to them in terms of beliefs, values, or interests. Homophily is a cornerstone of network analysis. It helps us understand and then explain the formation and structure of social networks, illustrating how shared preferences and affinities shape relational ties. In the context of fandom studies, homophily is especially relevant as it reveals how shared tastes for and interests in popular culture foster the creation of tightly knit fan communities. These networks of shared taste and interest amplify fandom's social dynamics. They underpin everything from collaborative content creation to the organization of conventions. Measuring and visualizing the nature, shape, and strength of these ties enables us to better understand how shared cultural interests drive online and offline interactions. Homophily also underscores how the conversations that fans have within fandom frame social expectations about how fans should read particular texts and images. However, as long as audience measurement tools are focused more on the attention of individual viewers rather than their homophiles and shared practices, the industry is going to make decisions blindly that can adversely impact the fan ecosystem.

Sam Ford (2010) describes, for example, how the audience for soap operas once extended across multiple generations of (mostly) women within the same family. In this case, the grandmother might have possessed the most extensive knowledge of how the story had evolved over time and, thus, might have been called upon to fill in the backstory that is not known by her daughter or granddaughter. Such extensive knowledge was deemed valuable given the fact that many American soap operas had run for decades on television and radio before that. However, several factors disrupted that ecology: first, younger women began to work during the day and used VCRs to record the programs to watch at night or stopped watching altogether. Second, new producers undervalued the importance of the older fans, gradually discontinuing the characters that held their loyalty and relying less on extended program histories. This neglect of senior fans proved nearly fatal to a genre that had once thrived on American television because these older fans were vital to the informational infrastructure of soap's audiences. In Ford's analysis, fans, even on the level of the family unit, are best understood as socially configured, with each fan's preferences being important to the viability of the program and for the persistence of its audience.

Star Trek and Worldcon

The media industries, contrary to their own claims, do not "create" fans; they court them. That is, in many cases, fandoms pre-exist particular media performers or texts, representing shared sets of interests and often pre-existing social communities. Fan attention is directed toward particular objects at specific moments in time; their interests may take them elsewhere when the producers no longer cater to their needs. A science fiction fan will seek out science fiction texts, and romance readers want romances. When a series such as *The Mandalorian* emerges, one that fulfills at least some of an existing fan group's needs, they turn their attention towards it; however, their commitment should not be taken for granted. They may walk away if the text is boring, if it does not continue to satisfy their needs, if the discussion around it becomes toxic, or for a range of other reasons.

Consider the case of *Star Trek*. When Gene Roddenberry wanted to build a base of support for his television series back in the mid-1960s, he showed the pilot episode to attendees at the World Science Fiction Convention (Worldcon) and asked for their help in building a larger audience. Making a tantalizing proposition to this group, which had been jaded by silly media science fiction series like the often ridiculous *Lost in Space*, he promised them a series that took the genre seriously. Worldcon had been held every year since 1939 and had a well-established community, traditions, and leadership. The convention was also in flux as more women were attending in the wake of a then fairly recent rise of feminist science fiction represented by writers like Ursula K. Le Guin and Joanna Russ. These women were battling sexual harassment from the mostly male, technophilic, and hard science fiction culture that had long considered Worldcon as their home base.

What we now think of as *Star Trek* fandom, then, was largely organized by these women who broke off from Worldcon and formed their own conventions, taking some practices from the old science fiction zine culture and giving it their own spin. One reason why, in the age of network communications, fandoms can emerge quickly in the age of network communications is because they are often constituted by fans who are already following a genre and are looking for promising new content around which to organize their ongoing conversations. Alternatively, they may be collections of those who feel dissatisfied with one series and are searching for something that better satisfies their yearnings.

Brand Loyalty and Migratory Audiences

In their 2009 book *Communities of Play*, game theorists Celia Pearce, Tom Boellstorf, and Bonnie Nardi offer an account of what we might call a migratory or nomadic audience. They explain,

> At the heart of this book is the story of one specific play community, members of the Uru Diaspora, a group of players cast out of an online game to become refugees. It is the story of the bonds they formed in spite of—indeed because of—this shared trauma, and about their tenacious determination to remain together and to reclaim and reconfigure their own unique group identity and culture. It is a story about the power of play to coalesce a community beyond the boundaries of the game in which it formed, and into the real world itself (Pearce, Boellstorf and Nardy, 2009, pp. 6-7).

Understanding fandoms in this way allows us to anticipate where fan interests might emerge as a result of tracing former patterns of behavior and earlier configurations of tastes and responding to them with both content and practices intended to make it easier for them to pursue their passions. From the perspective of the fans themselves, producers and brands need to remember that we are not <u>your</u> fans in the sense that you own us or that we are necessarily loyal to your products. Rather, you are the keepers of <u>our</u> beloved fan objects, at least for now.

In an era of expanding media options, fans may align temporarily with producers only as long as media makers or product producers provide entertainment that is meaningful and pleasurable to them and as long as these "powers that be" adopt policies and practices that are not antagonistic to their needs and desires. Some fan commitments—fanships—can, of course, last a lifetime: fans of the Los

Angeles Dodgers may remain Dodgers' fans seemingly from birth, be it because of family tradition or having grown out of a longstanding interest in sports. However, such lifelong commitments are relatively rare, given the churn of popular culture. One can become a Dodgers fan by moving to the region, following a player in fantasy sports, or choosing to align with a particular team because you follow a player who has been traded or you like their ethos.

Fandom studies start with the premise that fans are people who care passionately about some sector of popular culture, who creatively and critically engage with its products, and who actively share their passions with others. These interests may or may not translate into more consumption of cultural products, from media franchises to consumer brands. Much depends on how media producers and marketers respond to such engagement, whether fans are welcomed or belittled, incorporated or excluded, and this is the heart of what we are calling "fandom relations."

Fandom relations transpire in a world of networked communication that has fundamentally transformed the way some audiences engage with popular culture, fostering collaborative practices that extend well beyond the narrow bounds of passive consumption. Fan audiences share their experiences and insights with others, crafting fan theories, remixing media, and contributing to a vast ecosystem of fan-created content. Platforms such as social media provide spaces where fan audiences can form new audiences that connect, interpret, and expand upon media texts, often with the anticipation that others within the community will engage with their creations. Being a fan is no longer assumed to be a solitary activity; it can often become a collective endeavor that requires a networked environment. As a result, the technologically savvy fan audience wields powerful collective intelligence that empowers them to produce interpretations and creative outputs that continually enhance the cultural relevance of a vast range of media productions.

As we acknowledge the novel needs and innovative means by which networked fan audiences fill them, we begin to see how the collective work of fans often involves reconfiguring media texts. Whether it is answering a burning question, filling in a backstory or history, predicting a winner, or interpreting lyrics in light of knowledge of an artist, the dynamic intermixing of fascination for a fan object with frustration about its limitations drives much of the creative labor within fandom. The next chapter delves into this process, exploring how fans take what mass culture offers them and appropriate it, transforming mass cultural productions into fan objects that better reflect their own desires, identities, and social realities. Through this lens, we gain an enhanced understanding of how fandoms in contemporary culture act as both creative and critical forces.

CHAPTER 8:

Appropriation, Fascination, and Frustration: How Fandom Works

The formula for fandom is a complex mixture of appropriation, fascination, and frustration. Fans often engage with media in ways that go far beyond mere consumption and actively negotiate levels of engaged experience with the content they love. This chapter explores how fans, particularly those from marginalized groups, use fandom as a space to critically engage with media representations, reflecting on what resonates with them, what falls short, and what could be reimagined. Drawing from Stuart Hall's theory of cultural negotiation (Hall, 1980), we portray fandom as a social space where acceptance and rejection are not binary choices but part of an ongoing dialogue between fans and the cultural products they consume. Fans, through their engagement, construct customized interpretations of their own, sometimes producing alternative narratives or representations that better align with their desires, hopes, and worldviews.

As we progress through this chapter, we will explore how fans take mass-produced culture and transform it into something more personal and meaningful. Whether through fan fiction, fan art, or online discussions, fans retrofit existing media to meet their current needs and forward-looking expectations. In this sense, fandom functions as a kind of cultural re-appropriation, where fans stitch the individual squares of media texts into the vast quilt of popular culture through their interactions, transforming these texts into a part of both their identity and their repertoire of social expressions through the process of cutting and sewing.

This transformation further blurs the line between producer and consumer, with fans adding value to media texts by infusing them with their own interpretations, critiques, and extensions. As we examine fandom in its many forms—whether it be around TV shows, movies, sports, or even theme parks—this chapter will highlight how the processes of fascination and frustration fuel the active participation of fans, driving them to explore and expand upon the raw cultural materials provided by the media, sports, and entertainment industries.

Fandom's Central Admixture

Fandom often provides people, especially those from marginalized groups, a chance to think through the available media representations together, to discuss what they like and what they don't like, and often to produce alternative versions of their favorite characters that more perfectly reflect their desires, fantasies, hopes, and aspirations in regard to gender, sexuality, or race. In that sense, following Stuart Hall (1980), fandom is a space of negotiation, rarely either of simple acceptance or outright rejection of what is given.

We can say that fandom is born of a mixture of fascination and frustration. If fans were not fascinated with a particular media object, they would simply walk away, given the broad range of different media calling for their attention. Modern streaming media, for example, offers many more options than we could consume in our lifetime. Neil Postman (1985) warned that we were "amusing ourselves to death." Today, we might "Netflix and chill." But if the fans were not frustrated, they might consume what is given and be fully satisfied. Fans look at media texts as, to borrow a term from real estate, "fixer-uppers," whose foundations are strong, who have elements they find attractive, pleasurable, and meaningful, but where there are aspects left to explore, things missing they would like to see, plot developments they anticipate, or flaws in the representation that bug them.

Both individually and collectively, fans construct their own culture as a means of retrofitting what the creative industries offer them, of reimagining popular culture to more fully meet their needs. Indeed, Fandom Studies often makes a distinction between mass culture, culture that is mass produced, mass distributed, and mass consumed, and popular culture, culture that has been appropriated as a resource for the formation of our identities and expressions of our world view in everyday life. A song played on Top 40 radio is mass culture; that same song sung in the shower starts to become popular culture because of its selection and use as a resource for everyday life. When we sing it with our friends at a karaoke bar, it becomes a part of how we connect with others.

Fandom takes this process of appropriation further, suggesting how these elements borrowed from mass culture become popular as they form the basis for much more elaborate forms of cultural expression—say, a TikTok video. In that sense, television, music, and sports are ordinary—part of everyday life—and they belong as much to consumers as they do to producers, since fans and other consumers often produce meanings or direct attention or identify uses in ways that increase the value of the mass media materials being offered to them in the marketplace.

Cultural Appropriation

Today, we often discuss appropriation in negative terms. The phrase "cultural appropriation" is often used to discuss cases where a dominant group raids a minority culture and lays claim to their cultural practices. The term surfaces, for example, in debates about dressing as a geisha or a bandito for Halloween (Hua, 2009). However, fandom studies starts with the premise that all creativity builds on the foundations of what came before.

It is a matter of power. Many different kinds of consumers are forced to appropriate the products of mass production to make them into resources for resistance and survival, to ensure they satisfy unfulfilled needs. Cultural appropriation also often involves powerful groups taking, without permission and often without comprehension, forms of culture from less powerful groups. We may well disagree about where the borders between the two lie, and many critiques of cultural appropriation involve sloppy thinking that implies one group may exclusively possess some form of culture or that cultures are somehow pure and untainted by outside influences. The best writers in the cultural studies tradition—George Lipsitz (1997), for example—teach us that most forms of mass culture have hybrid origins, mixing and matching different cultural traditions in order to broaden their potential markets.

In a recent essay, Sangita Shresthova (2025) digs into the debates around

Fascination and Frustration in Fandom Landscapes

Although it has traditionally been associated primarily with media texts like TV shows, movies, or books, the notion of fandom has expanded its horizons to encapsulate a multitude of commercial domains. This expansion suggests that the concept of fandom is not confined to media alone but is a broader phenomenon stemming from a human connection to various consumption objects, be they music, sports, brands, videogames, or even theme parks. Our core argument throughout this series is that the heart of fandom beats wherever there is passion, desire, and an underlying bond between the consumer and the consumed.

For example, music fans are not merely aficionados of appealing melodies or poetic lyrics; they resonate with the emotions, memories, and experiences evoked by particular songs, musicians, genres, composers, historical eras, dance movements, and so on. Whether fans are attending concerts, participating in album launches, or deconstructing the meaning of lyrics, their engagement goes beyond passive listening. They may be fascinated by an artist's vocal prowess or the depth of lyrics, or they may just want to move with the beat.

Spotify has over 100 million songs and adds almost 50,000 songs every day. Yet, among this mountain of sounds, fans likely yearn for more—the desire for a specific collaboration, the longing for the return of a past music style, passion for a relatively unknown artist, or the simple desire to insert themselves closer into the music, to feel it more. Along comes TikTok. The social platform is a place where music aficionados host global singalongs, launch song contests, or even propel a previously unknown track to chart-topping status. TikTok is a place where appreciation meets innovation, as fans add their unique narratives to the mix, showcasing both their love for the

cultural appropriation and Bollywood dance, suggesting that Bollywood across its history has brought together many different choreographic traditions, merging classical Indian dance with influences from disco, hip-hop, and even K-pop, through active borrowing and sometimes by inviting in choreographers from Eastern Europe or America for collaboration. Bollywood has also grown through cultural associations on campuses around the world, where fans from the West have danced with those who engaged with Bollywood films growing up in India or the South Asian diaspora. She argues that the attempt to preserve a "pure" and "authentic" Bollywood untouched by outside influences is misguided under these circumstances and threatens to render the dance form static, cutting it off from stylistic growth and spread to other communities, both of which have contributed to its growth through the years. She acknowledges that the determination of what constitutes unwanted cultural appropriation is particular to specific circumstances and may require the development of an ethics of appropriation. Shrestova is not seeking to close off discussions of cultural appropriation but rather to shift the terms upon which they are framed.

original sounds and their vision of what it can be. More and more songs are designed to have the right beats and the right refrains to play well in the small bursts required for success on TikTok. And popular performers like Lil' Naz become shrewd at calculating what it will take to get TikTok fans to take up his music and pass it along to others in their consumer tribe (Arrietta, 2021).

For many sports fans, their home stadium is a temple and the game is a ritual. Their fandom transcends the mere act of watching a match to see who will win. Layers of fascination spike the sports fan experience with appreciation for the athleticism of athletes, behind-the-scenes stories of intrigue and inspiration, coaching and game strategy, or the camaraderie of teams. Along with the fascination, frustration is always just around the corner, as when the team loses a big game, when strategies fall flat, or when beloved athletes are injured or retire.

Fantasy sports leagues allowed fans to step into the shoes of managers and strategists, just as TikTok granted music fans a new degree of immersion in musical experiences. These platforms allowed fans to craft whole new teams from existing ones, strategize based on sports league rules, monitor and cheer for individual player performances, and predict the outcomes of novel matchups, thus integrating their deep knowledge of the game with a hands-on interactive—and, often, gambling-based— experience.

Consumption experiences become arenas for the passions of fandom as well. Recently, a mechanical keyboard fandom has emerged that celebrates and appreciates the tactile and auditory experiences that older-style mechanical keyboards offer. Education and knowledge sharing are a big part of this fandom, with many members creating guides, tutorials, and videos to help others. This educational outreach is particularly evident on platforms like the 1.2 million-member r/MechanicalKeyboards subreddit and on YouTube, where creators like Taeha Types showcase builds, reviews, and more for more than 500,000 subscribers.

Participants in the mechanical keyboard fandom will purchase or craft keycaps and switches, create custom builds and modifications, and even design their own keyboard layouts. The keyboards become akin to work tools that are also personalized pieces of art. Because of the niche nature of these activities, members will often organize group purchases so that they can meet minimum order quantities from manufacturers. The collective approach not only ensures everyone gets the parts they want, but it also fosters a sense of unity and collaboration. Representing their own unique set of values and ethos, mechanical keyboard enthusiasts embrace brands like Corsair and Ducky while also expressing frustration over certain product changes or missed features, very much like how fans see potential "fixer-uppers" in media texts.

Theme park fandom (Williams, 2020) provides yet another example of a group drawn in by a service that transcends mere recreation, becoming a type of alternate reality where beautiful fantasies come to life. Theme park fandoms often focus on the intricate world-building and imaginative craftsmanship, the adrenaline rush of rides, and the sense of nostalgia and freedom these special places can provide. Although fascinated with these immersive experiences, theme park fandoms voice frustrations that arise from the longing for a particular canceled ride, changes to beloved attractions, or the anticipation of new park sections. In a digital age, this mix of admiration and annoyance has evolved with fans creating and sharing detailed ride-along videos for rides that no longer exist, offering memories of their past experiences, and reviewing past and upcoming attractions. These digital artifacts serve as both a testament to their experiences and a guide for others looking to embark on similar journeys, whether real, imagined, or reconstructed in memory.

These participatory fan dynamics, epitomized by the duality of fascination and frustration, appear across the various domains of fandom we explore in this series, from music and sports to consumer products, theme parks, news, and more. Each category of fans, although unique in their specific engagements, shares a universal pattern of deep attraction coupled with a desire for more. Whether we are discussing a media text, a melodious track, a thrilling game, a cherished brand, or a nostalgic theme park ride, fans view them as universes unto themselves, experiences with boundless potential They often seek to dive deeper into their worlds, immersing themselves in imaginative admixtures of what is offered and what might be.

CHAPTER 9:
Transmedia Audiences and Authors

n our last chapter, we explored how fandom often operates from a position of appropriation, fascination, and frustration—fans taking the media they love, making them their own, and also grappling with their limitations or disappointments. This chapter builds upon that foundation by examining a new frontier in the relationship between fans and media: transmedia storytelling and its role in shaping modern fan culture. We shift from the framework of classical Hollywood cinema, which emphasized self-contained, easily digestible films, toward an understanding of today's media landscape, where popular narratives stretch across multiple platforms, demanding deeper engagement from fans.

Here, we will focus on how modern media franchises like Disney's Marvel Cinematic Universe are designed with transmedia consumers in mind—spectators who are viewed as active participants moving through a sprawling, interconnected universe of content. These transmedia fans are not merely observers and watchers; they actively engage with stories through television shows, comics, social media, and even games. The media they consume requires them to make meaningful connections across platforms, and the pleasure of the experience often lies in the discovery of hidden references, the accumulation of knowledge, and participation in a broader fan community.

By examining how the media environment has shifted from classical Hollywood's singular, standalone narratives to the intricate, multi-platform storytelling of today, we will also look at how this shift reshapes the relationship between fans and creators. Figures like Quentin Tarantino and Ronald D. Moore, who cultivate engaged fan bases across multiple media, highlight how modern authorship has become a process that is both collaborative and dispersed. As we delve into transmedia authorship and fandom, we will also explore further ways that the lines between creators and audiences blur, allowing for richer, more participatory fan experiences that challenge traditional notions of storytelling and consumption.

This chapter, then, is a deep dive into the transmedia landscape and the new kinds of spectatorship it demands. It builds directly on the dynamics discussed earlier—how fans appropriate, remix, and engage with media—and takes these ideas further by exploring the ways in which today's media culture encourages even more complex interactions between fans, creators, and the stories they love.

From Classical Hollywood Spectators to Transmedia Consumers

Let's think a bit more about how the producer's mental models of the intended audience shape the encoding process. A good starting point might be to consider some statements filmmaker Martin Scorsese made about Marvel films and their fans. Referring to an interview he gave to *Empire*, a British magazine on science fiction and fantasy, Scorsese (2019) wrote in *The New York Times*:

> {Marvel films] seem to me to be closer to theme parks than they are to movies as I've known and loved them throughout my life, and. . . in the end, I don't think

they're cinema....I know that if I were younger, if I'd come of age at a later time, I might have been excited by these pictures and maybe even wanted to make one myself. But I grew up when I did and I developed a sense of movies — of what they were and what they could be — that was as far from the Marvel universe as we on Earth are from Alpha Centauri (n.p.).

Scorsese had much to say about the meaningfulness of classical genre films, the current production environment, the shift from theatrical presentation to streaming platforms, but for the moment, we can ask what notions of spectatorship underlie Scorsese's sense that the Marvel films are not "cinema" as he has understood it.

The films Scorsese uses as his primary examples represent an era known as "Classical Hollywood Cinema" (Bordwell, Staiger, Thompson, 1985). During this period, the average American went to see movies in theaters 1-2 times per week, and the most hardcore cinephiles went more often. They developed a critical understanding of stars, filmmakers, studio styles, and, most of all, genres, reading genre films against each other to identify the distinctive voice of their directors in what became known as the auteur theory (Grant, 2008). Classical Hollywood Cinema adopted a series of codes and conventions that made it easy for audiences to comprehend what was going on. Their aesthetic was—as Scorsese notes—centered on characters, their goals, the obstacles they confronted, and their emotional journey through the narrative.

The classical movie was understood as a self-contained work, so there was a strong expectation of closure or resolution in the final moments. Everything required to understand the action was on the screen, and the most important information was repeated three or more times as part of this larger system of orienting the spectator.

Historians of the book talk about the difference between intensive reading (say, people reading the Bible over and over) and extensive reading (reading across a much broader range of available texts). We might say that Classical Hollywood depended on extensive reading, as consumers came each week expecting a new story and new characters, whereas contemporary Hollywood often assumes more intensive reading, as people identify stories and characters they would like to spend extended periods of time with, digging deeper into their backstories and anticipating future developments. They watch these titles again on streaming or DVD, freeze-framing, slow advancing, and closed-captioning to wring as much from the experience as possible. However, there are extensive aspects of contemporary reading practices since transmedia practices assume that works are not self-sufficient but operate in relation to a larger web of intertexts and paratexts.

The Marvel films are made with a very different conception of the audience —a model some associate with transmedia entertainment. Transmedia refers to structured relationships amongst and across different media. Transmedia is an adjective in search of a noun, and when applied to storytelling, it refers to a process of spreading aspects of the story across multiple media (Jenkins, 2008).

If the Classical Hollywood spectator was assumed to be watching a discrete film with a clearly demarcated beginning, middle, and ending, all consumed in a single sitting, the spectator of a transmedia franchise is assumed to be encountering multiple texts and making meaningful connections between them. From the start, Marvel Comics told serialized stories, each monthly title organized around the adventures of a single character. They featured crossover appearances in each other's comic books and coordinated events that unfolded across all of the Marvel titles. The result was a sense of the Marvel universe that expanded with each new story and publication. The reader was assumed to possess a strong recall of the continuity of this ever-expanding narrative, its backstory, and the characters. Within any given issue, the character might be relatively flat and static. Still, the fan's understanding of the character depended on impressions formed over time and comparisons drawn across various storylines. Contrary to Scorsese's statement, these fans are still drawn to characters as the primary vehicle through which they relate to these films.

The MCU assumes, as a starting point, a committed and passionate viewer. They do not assume film fans have read the comics, and so the majority of these films have started with origin stories. Still, they do expect that many, if not most, spectators will consistently consume their films (and perhaps other related works, television series, games, and so forth). The films are not complete and self-contained; they are full of rabbit holes (which encourage us to dig deeper) and easter eggs (tossed-off rewards for fan mastery), and what limited closure there is at the end of the film is followed by post-credit scenes hinting at new developments in the universe, which will play out in future, interrelated motion picture series.

Scorsese (2019) continues, "It was about characters—the complexity of people and their contradictory and sometimes paradoxical natures, the way they can hurt one another and love one another and suddenly come face to face with themselves" (n.p.). Scorsese refers to the character development in a single film that often occurs through bits of dialogue delivered in the midst of action sequences. MCU fans, much like comic fans before them, accumulate a deeper understanding of those characters across multiple adventures. Fan fiction writers, by the thousands, have used their understanding of those characters as the basis for further explorations of the choices the characters make, the codes that govern them, and the pain they feel over loss and destruction. The superhero, in this way, becomes as fully developed a personage as the Westerner or the gangster in the films Scorsese has celebrated and emulated throughout his career.

The process, then, is cumulative. The more Marvel content we consume, the better we understand the nuances of what we are watching. To fully understand *Dr. Strange and the Multiverse of Madness,* for example, one would need to understand the titular character's backstory from earlier Dr. Strange and Avengers movies, have followed the shift of Scarlet Witch towards the dark side on the *Wanda/Vision* television series, know about America Garcia from her own comic book series, and grasp the properties of the multiverse as explained on the *Loki* or *What If?* television series, to cite just a few examples.

Moreover, the new spectator is assumed to be plugged into a social network that can provide them with information they may lack: they can look up any character they do not recognize on Wikipedia; they may follow an ongoing discussion on Reddit or some other platform; they may trade hot takes on Facebook or TikTok; they may see memes that underline major plot points; and they may read press coverage that tries to identify and decipher embedded details known only to the most hardcore fan. The classical Hollywood spectator of Scorsese's formative years engaged with the films in a public setting, laughing together or gasping together in response to the action. However, the new franchise films depend on the expanded cognitive capacities of a network of hunters and gatherers [Mittel's (2016) forensic fandom] who demand greater complexity from their entertainment and who seek out information anywhere and everywhere, in ways that become fodder for their conversations with others.

Scorsese may well be correct that these films do not operate according to the old classical rules; rather, they are a new form of "cinema" that serves the needs and desires of a new kind of spectator. We map the differences in these two paradigms of cinematic spectatorship in Table 9.1.

Classical Cinema	Transmedia Franchises
Works are self-contained	Works are interconnected
Everything repeated three times to ensure audience comprehension	Easter eggs and rabbit holes reward viewer mastery of secondary texts
Meanings must be accessible on single viewing	Meanings may be discovered through close and multiple readings at home
Works designed for individual comprehension	Works designed to be consumed by networks of forensic fans
Character development across a film	Character information is accumulated across texts and elaborated upon by fan debates and fan fiction
Extensive reading	Both intensive and extrinsic reading

Table 9.1: Comparing Classical and Transmedia Cinema

Transmedia Authorship

Scorsese fears that the corporate coordination required for this new style of cinema may foreclose the distinctive voices of auteurs; however, we might consider an example of a transmedia author, Quintin Tarantino (Jenkins, forthcoming). From the start, Tarantino has often made in-joke references to other popular culture works, such as the debate about the meaning of Madonna's song "Like a Virgin" in *Reservoir Dogs*, the pastiche of genres in the film *Kill Bill*, or the ways Tarantino utilizes the music of Enrico Morricone (*The Good, the Bad, and the Ugly*) across many of his motion pictures. Moreover, as the owner of Los Angeles' New Beverly Cinema, he programs a range of films that inspired him in anticipation of the release of his new titles, often discussing these other movies in blogs and podcasts.

Tarantino has built up a taste community that understands his films' citations and homages. He regularly appears as a guest, helping to dissect his works on the *Pure Cinema* podcast, which he uses to promote his theater, or the *Video Archives* podcast, which he hosts with longtime collaborator Roger Avery to discuss movies they recall from their youth working at a video store. Here, we see Tarantino constructing his status as an author in conversation with other film-makers and across a range of different media contexts.

With *Once Upon a Time in Hollywood*, a film about a transitional moment in cinema history, he took these ideas even further by writing a novelization of the film that significantly expands our understanding of the core characters and their motivations. On the *Video Archives* podcast, he and his co-hosts announced the death of the film's fictional protagonist, Rick Dalton, and offered a retrospective of his works, some of which were mentioned in the film and some of which fill in gaps before or following the movie's events, expanding the timeline. Rumors persist that Tarantino may oversee the development of a new series of *Lancer*, which, within *Once Upon a Time in Hollywood* narrative, Dalton guest stars. He produced a range of period-appropriate advertisements, musical appearances, and other media that were shown before the film in some locations and were included as DVD extras.

Here, Tarantino depends on the audience's pleasure in making connections across the various texts that constitute the world of *Once Upon a Time in Hollywood*. All of this assumes that a knowledgeable audience, one that has done its homework, can read as deeply as it wants into the associated texts and has an appreciation for Tarantino's genre mixing, cross-referencing, and metadiscourse on the history of popular media.

While transmedia frames provide a new way to consider the content strategies required to serve fan audiences, they may also reshape how we think about the relationship between fans and authors, as demonstrated in our example of Tarantino above. In recent years, there has been a significant shift in the cultural status of television—from the early conception of television as "the vast wasteland" in the 1960s to more recent formulations of "quality television," often described in "cinematic" or "novelistic" terms starting in the 1990s (Mittell, 2008). This discourse around quality arguably started with Viewers for Quality Television (Brower, 1992), founded in 1984 in an effort to save *Cagney and Lacey* from cancelation. This fan organization sought to protect some of its members' favorite programs (such as *Frank's Place, Quantum Leap, Sports Night* and *Party of Five*) from cancellation by making the case that quality shows attracted a demographic of viewers that were especially desired by advertisers and should thus be protected despite low ratings. Arguments linking "quality" television with upscale demographics were used by HBO—"It's not television! It's HBO!" (Jenkins and Jenkins, 2020), and later by streaming services to justify the move from advertising-supported broadcast to what was formerly called "pay TV" or subscription-based services.

Part of making this case was the argument that television—especially drama and genre programs—was becoming a more personal medium by the 1980s and 1990s. It is difficult to identify the author of a television series compared to motion pictures or other mediums because of the reliance on writers' rooms for the majority of shows rather than single writers and the fact that directors tend to move from show to show rather than actively oversee a single television series. In recent times, the "showrunner" has emerged as a new position in the production process, one that fuses the responsibilities of head writer and executive producer and is intended to ensure the consistency of the production over time.

Performing Authorship: Ronald D. Moore and *Outlander*

The position of the "showrunner" has become that of a public spokesperson for their television series and, thus, the person who performs and embodies authorship for the fans. We might consider them as performing what Michel Foucault (1999) described as the functions of the author:

1. The author serves as a principle of classification, helping to organize the relations between texts.
2. The author serves as a principle of explanation.
3. The author functions as a sign of value since only certain texts are read as authored.

In fact, "performing" is the operative word since they so often embody these functions, staging them for fans and articulating them directly to shape how we consume and interpret their works. Today, we have access to more authorial discourse than ever before, as filmmakers perform the role of authors across a range of media. Fans generally know these showrunners through public appearances at San Diego Comic-Con and other conventions, interviews in the press, appearances on ancillary materials—such as DVD extras or commentary—and their active presence on social media. Fans know their personalities, histories, and philosophies, and, as such, they attribute much of the meaning they find in the programs to these showrunners.

Citing Peter Jackson's appearance in promotional materials around the *Lord of the Rings* trilogy, Jonathan Gray (2010) notes that such promotional materials not only serve as marketing but also position audiences to read the films in certain ways. Moreover, he suggests that it situates the fans as insiders who know the behind-the-scenes decision-making process shaping their favorite movies and serves to extend credit to other production personnel who helped to make the work "special."

Let's consider one example of how the showrunner—in this case, Ronald D. Moore (Starz, 2014 4)—performs these functions within the contemporary media environment. Moore began his career working on *Star Trek: The Next Generation* and attracted fan attention as the showrunner for *Battlestar Galactica*. He followed this stint by becoming the showrunner for *Outlander*, a show based on Diana Gabaldon's romance and fantasy novels that primarily attracted a female audience. Seeking to draw some of his existing male fans to this new and different context, Moore participated in a promotional video for the series, where he explained his philosophy and how it fits into his broader body of work, thus performing each of Foucault's author functions in turn:

> I respond to interesting characters and situations and try to portray them as truthfully as I can and try to make the world they inhabit as truthful as I can. All of the shows I have done are period pieces; just some of them have been in the future. It is still creating a world that does not exist for the audience so the production challenges are similar in that you can't go out on the street and shoot… I am a firm believer that if you are going to take the audience on this fantastic journey, you really have to ground it; you have to make them believe it is really happening, so that when they take that big leap, they are really going to go there (Starz, 2014).

Here, Moore uses his reputation as a gifted worldbuilder to link *Outlander* and *Battlestar Galactica*, stressing a particular production approach and relationship to the audience he wants to achieve. This rationale allows us to classify *Outlander* as a Moore series, even though it is deeply grounded in the work of another author, Diana

Gabaldon, who wrote the original book series. In the video, *Battlestar Galactica* is never directly referenced but is understood to be part of what he means when he describes his body of work as historical fiction set in the future. Pay attention to his use of the second person, "you," throughout the quote above, to make the listener identify with the showrunner and blur the boundaries between what he is responsible for and what is done by other collaborators, such as costume designers, production designers, and special effects artists. As such, he promotes himself as the primary agent to whom we can attribute causation for these features, and his professionalism becomes a central value in how audiences evaluate his productions. "If the world feels false or if they can tell you are winking at them along the way, I think the audience instinctively pulls back and they will not give of themselves as deeply as they will if they believe in the entire environ-ment" (Starz, 2014).

Transferring Authorship: Robert Kirkman and *The Walking Dead*

Once established, this performance of authorship can be trans-ferred to other agents, as Robert Kirkman does in another Making of video (IGN, 2016), where he introduces the team behind the *Walking Dead* videogames, Telltale, and explains how they are linked to the television series and comic books, both of which he oversees as the primary author. He contrasts Michonne, a character he created for the comics, with Len and Clem, the protagonists of earlier games set in the *Walking Dead* universe, who originated with Telltale writers.

> Michonne as a character is probably a lot more capable and attuned to this world than Lee and Clem had been even towards the end of their games, just because she has lived in this world so long. So what that means is that there's an even bigger action element in her game than in the

other two. There's a tremendous amount of backstory and character baggage that comes with Michonne just because she's existed in more than a hundred issues of the comic book series at the point when she arrives in the game so the player is so much more familiar with her and knows so much more about her than they know about Lee and Clem when they start those games (IGN, 2006, n.p.).

Kirkman discusses the plot logic that opened a chapter for Michonne that he was unable to represent in the comics and wanted to tell through another medium:

95 percent of the journey she goes on is not seen and that's why I thought this Telltale game was a great opportunity to show that stuff. I think Michonne is such a strong character and so much is going on with her emotionally and I think that's something that the TellTale games handle really well with emotion... I just thought it would be a really great opportunity to do a chapter in the Telltale saga that focused on one of the characters in the comic books and also told the story of a big chunk of her life that was missing in the comics (IGN, 2006, n.p.).

Kirkman presents himself as the source of the story, as the visionary behind the world, as the authority on the characters and the backstories; however, as he discusses how the games intersect the comics and the series, Kirkman gradually introduces what he sees as the strong points of the Telltale team, their ability to create games that explore the emotional lives of the characters, and then signals his transfer of authority to them. He continues: "I really trust the team at Telltale... I gave them a block of time, I threw in a couple of characters that I thought should be featured, but for the most part, I let Telltale run wild. While it does follow significant directions about what I wanted to see happen in Michonne's time off, there are definitely a lot of surprises along the way, even for me. It all counts. It's all real" (ibid).

If you consider Kirkman as an author, he is authorizing the games as part of the canon of the story ("It all counts. It's all real.") Rhetorically, then, this is an adept performance of transmedia authorship. Keep in mind that these moves were no doubt deliberated with the public relations team as part of their larger fan relations strategy before Kirkman was sat in front of a camera or this footage was edited for its release on the internet.

The FanBoy Auteur

Suzanne Scott (2012) has written about Moore, Kirkman, and others in terms of what she calls the "fanboy auteur," a rhetorical strategy where a media creator claims allegiance with the fans against the "powers that be" and uses this rhetoric to claim authenticity for the works they produce. Scott writes, "Fanboy auteurs are relatable because of their fan credentials, which are narrativized and (self) promoted as an integral part of their appeal as a transmedia interpreter of audiences. Some anecdotal evidence suggests that their rise to professional/creator status is a product of their fan identity, while others frame their conflicted identity as creator/fan as augmenting their ability to understand what fans want, thus making them more equipped to cater to fans" (Scott, 2012, p. 44). When Scott ascribes to such figures "power to demarcate primary and secondary texts, inducting some transmedia texts into the canon and excluding others," she is gesturing to Foucault's analysis of the author function. Here, we will continue to focus on television showrunners as an illustration of this process, but others, including Scott, have extended the category to include filmmakers and other categories of media-makers (Scott, 2013; Scott, 2019; Salter and Stanfil, 2020).

Damon Lindelof, one of the showrunners for *Lost*, describes the tensions in the audience's expectations regarding authorship:

> The question that Carleton [Cuse] and I get asked by far, over any other mythological question about the show, is: 'are you making it up as you go along?' When people ask us that question, they want the answer to be, 'Absolutely not!'… However, they also say to us, 'Do you ever go on the boards and listen to what the fans have to say?' and they want the answer to that question to be 'Absolutely yes!' Now these two things are in direct opposition to each other. (Jenkins, 2010, n.p.)

These questions display the paradoxes of authorship within a serialized medium such as television that evolves over a prolonged production and distribution cycle. What fans seek from authors (but also reserve for themselves) is the protection of continuity; what they claim mostly for themselves through various fan works is the role of a generator of multiplicity, the production of diverse accounts of what motivates the characters, how to fill in gaps in the narrative, and how to reconstruct backstory. According to Jenkins (2012, p. 55), what distinguishes the fanboy auteur from his predecessors is "his heightened awareness of the reading process, his knowledge of the culture work fans do to create meaning and value around the cultural shards provided by the entertainment industry."

The fanboy auteur strategy often requires the splitting of two roles—that of the author and of the "powers that be," the corporate forces to whom all controversial or "bad" decisions get ascribed. As Jenkins (2012) writes, "Being a fanboy auteur creates sympathy from the audience but also raises expectations" (p. 58). Splitting these roles, at least rhetorically, allows the showrunner to remain an ally of the audience, even if they sometimes have to explain the commercial reasons why certain decisions were made. This strategy also allows the showrunner to ally with the fans on "Save Our Shows" campaigns when the series is under threat of cancellation—again, splitting the producers from the networks in discussing how decisions were made. In the earliest Save Our Show campaign on behalf of the original *Star Trek*, Susan Sackett, who was producer Gene Roddenberry's assistant, was a central conduit to the fan organizers and was widely known within the community. However, today, showrunners directly reach out to fans via social media to encourage them to write letters, watch the show, and do other supportive actions, as was the case with more recent campaigns on behalf of *Timeless* or *One Day at a Time*.

The Fanboy Auteur as a "Brand"

Anastasia Salter and Mel Stanfill (2020) further expanded on the concept of the fanboy auteur (and added the concept of the "fangirl auteur") in *A Portrait of the Auteur as Fanboy*. Declaring the fanboy auteur as a "brand" or "function" as much as it is a biographical figure, they conducted rich and nuanced case studies of the discourses surrounding figures such as Stephen Moffat, Kevin Smith, Joss Whedon, Zack Snyder, Ryan Coogler and others, considering the ways "fanboy auteur" discourses have often been used to contain fan voices and "correct" fan interpretation rather than to represent a voice for fans within the production process.

The modern showrunner performs Foucault's functions of the author through savvy use of transmedia promotion—recording "making of" videos or post-episode commentary as tools to shape the audience's perceptions of the series. These meta-segments are part of the transmedia franchise but operate on a different register, shaping our interpretation of the episodes, characters, and worlds by seeming to reveal something of the thinking behind their production. Moore, for example, produced an audio commentary for every episode of *Battlestar Galactica*, often directing our attention, for example, to elements of the mise en scène we might otherwise not have noticed and how they fit into the story's world. He might also share roads not taken—plot turns that were rejected or sequences cut from the aired episode—which might extend the story in interesting new directions. He might also plant hints and encourage us to anticipate future episodes by speculating about what might happen next.

These segments may seem authentic, natural, and intimate, helping us to get to know the author better; however, above all, they are constructing and performing the author across multiple media, including convention appearances, along lines already worked through by the promotional team. This transmedia nonfic-tion content allows the showrunner to assert claims anchoring him as an author in a system noted for its dispersed and collaborative mode of production, as Moore encourages us to make classifications that link *Outlander* to *Battlestar Galactica* and other projects on which he worked (while also rendering less visible other projects on which he worked). Second, these transmedia materials offer a form of explanation for why certain choices were made and not others. Finally, these segments can be understood as making bids for value and laying claim to status, as television has become understood as an authored medium worth respecting for its quality alongside motion pictures or novels. These performances of authorship con-stitute moments largely under the control of the production team and thus are designed to perform their rhetorical and functional goals. They are, in short, promotional materials intended not only to get us to consume certain media texts but also to shape our interpretation of them (Gray, 2010).

Skimmers, Dippers and Divers

As the above examples suggest, the emergence of transmedia logics of production and promotion has also responded to shifts in the way television operates, shifts that have placed greater emphasis on facilitating and sustaining the growth of fandom around particular media properties. In *Spreadable Media*, Henry and his co-authors Joshua Green and Sam Ford (2013, p. 116) chart the shift of American television from an appointment-based model to an engagement-based model:

> Under the appointment-based model, committed viewers arrange their lives to be home at a certain time to watch their favorite programs. Content is produced and distributed primarily to attract this attention at a certain time—viewership, which can be predicted and subsequently metered and sold to advertisers for profit... By contrast, engagement-based models see the audience as a collection of active agents whose labor may generate alternative forms of market value. This model places a premium on audiences willing to pursue content across multiple channels, as viewers access television on their own schedule... Such models value the spread of media texts as those engaged audiences are more likely to recommend, discuss, research, pass along, and even generate new media in response.

A striking feature of this new transmedia system is the emergence of specialized companies (Campfire, Starlite Media, Chaotic Good, The Alchemists) that advise major franchises on how to promote their properties in ways where the lines between promotion and storytelling are significantly blurred. We might also want to include more specialized subcontractors such as Telltale, the game company mentioned above, as working with *The Walking Dead* to extend the series into that medium.

Campfire, for example, a company that has done immersive and transmedia campaigns for properties such as *True Blood, Game of Thrones, The Man in the High Castle, The Purge,* and *Westworld,* was created by filmmakers who cut their teeth on *The Blair Witch Project,* long considered a high water mark for the marketing of a low-budget horror movie via digital media. Steve Coulson, Campfires Creative Director, described the company as "creating a stage for fans to walk out on and create their own parts" through initiatives such as inviting top chef Tom Collecio to run a food truck showcasing the foods of the imaginary realm Westeros for the launch of *Game of Thrones* or staging an immersive game where visitors enter the Western-themed amusement park Westworld (from the show of the same name) and interact with actors improvising the role of the androids.

Coulson has suggested that their efforts to engage transmedia audiences assume access to social media, whereby local experiences are transmitted to a larger audience, and also assume that viewers will bring different degrees of knowledge and commitment to the programs they promote.

> We call it Skimmers, Dippers, and Divers, and it's more about how much you as a fan want to get involved. If you imagine an upside-down pyramid, Skimmers are at the top. A Skimmer has a passing interest; they make up the biggest percentage, but they're the least engaged. Then at the tip of the pyramid, there's the Divers, and these are the hardcore fans, they're the people who cosplay—anything you give them, they'll peel it apart for authenticity. Divers are a really small part of your audience, but they do have

a disproportionate impact because they're the evangelists. The middle layer are the Dippers—they will engage, will tell their friends about it, will discuss it on social. They're not as hardcore, but they want to participate. When we design experiences, we want to make sure that we're creating things that all three of those strata will respond to, but especially the Dippers. It's easy to do something too deep for them or too shallow that it won't give them the tools to share (Akitunde, 2023, n.p.).

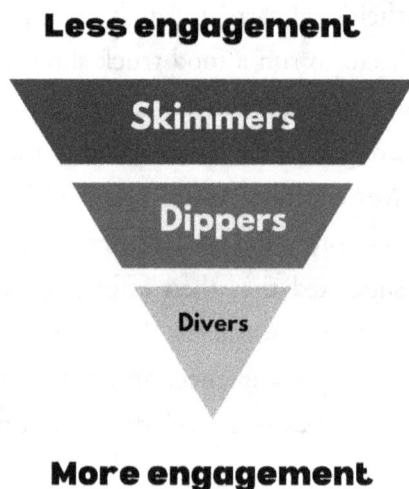

Less engagement

Skimmers

Dippers

Divers

More engagement

Figure 9.3: Differing Fan Engagement Segments: Skimmers, Dippers, and Divers

According to Campfire's model (Akitunde, 2023), transmedia strategies allow for the development of different kinds of content for audiences who want various degrees of immersion into and engagement with the story world. As we illustrate in Figure 9.3, the Divers represent the most hardcore fans (the ones we discuss most fully across *Frames of Fandom*); however, we need to remember that more casual forms of engagement are more widespread across the general audience. Campfire's campaigns imagine hardcore fans (Divers) actively and consciously transmitting information to a more diffused and casual audience of Dippers and Skimmers. Often, they start this process by sending special gifts to known influencers who use their status and social media channels to draw in a wider array of interested fans, and they create rewards to encourage Dippers to become Divers. The caution about assuming too deep a level of knowledge and engagement is a pragmatic one. Marvel has found ways to reward the Divers, who take pleasure in their background appreciation of Easter eggs and may pursue rabbit holes that lead them across media and into engaged discussions with others as they explore various fan theories. Similarly, secondary materials, such as web videos, may offer chances to dig even deeper

The Diver may swim circles around the other spectators. As Coulson explained, "The key is to start from the Dipper layer. We want to give somebody something that they'll enjoy, but they don't really need to do homework to enjoy. But then we'll go back and go, What easter eggs can we hide in plain sight? We don't want it to be distracting or for it to become hieroglyphs on the wall that people need to decipher to move forward" (ibid).

Richard Bartle (n.d.) proposed a typology for different forms of gamers that also describes the ways they support the interests of other classes of gamers, which was widely embraced within the games industry. We have yet to fully develop an ecology of transmedia fans that might guide future developments; however, Campfire's approach offers a rich starting point. The idea of designing for different levels of fan engagement contrasts sharply with the one-size-fits-all address of the kinds of films Scorsese preferred.

As we've seen throughout this chapter, the rise of transmedia storytelling marks a significant shift in how audiences engage with media. Unlike the self-contained films of Classical Hollywood, today's transmedia franchises create sprawling, interconnected narratives that require active audience engagement to decipher, decode, and fully enjoy. Fans in transmedia spaces become like detectives and researchers, decoding Easter eggs, tracking character arcs across platforms, and engaging with other fans online. This level of participation fosters a deeper emotional connection to the material and also turns audiencing into a collaborative experience where fans play a role in their fan object's ongoing trajectory rather than simply consuming it. The success of transmedia franchises depends on fans' willingness to engage across media, whether it be movies, television, video games, or social media.

In the next chapter, we will shift our focus from the transmedia worlds that fans navigate to the interpretive practices that shape how they engage with these narratives. As we move from looking at fandom to considering interpretive communities, we will explore how different conceptions of the audience affect not only how stories are told but also how they are experienced. We will discover how engagement, rather than content alone, has become the defining measure of success in the entertainment industry, and how communities of fans and readers eagerly work together to construct shared meanings from the media products they consume. This transition from fandom to broader audience dynamics will help us further unpack how culture is produced, circulated, and understood in today's rapidly changing media environment.

CHAPTER 9:

Audiences, Readers, and Interpretive Communities

As we saw in our example of the contrast between the spectators of Classical Hollywood cinema and contemporary transmedia audiences in the previous chapter, different industry conceptions of the audience have consequences on all aspects of cultural products, including how (and if) they tell stories, what they look and sound like, how they reach the market, and how their success is measured.

Today, we are told that "content is king," but the phrase is misleading since content literally means that which is contained, as in the contents of a bottle or a table of contents, while transmedia "content" is rarely contained, not in a single place or on one platform.

It is more accurate to say that "engagement is the central currency" of the entertainment industry in the way that attention alone once sufficed. In an age of fragmented audiences and expanding media production, success is measured in terms of how many people you can get to care about the media you produce. Engagement, in turn, is determined in part by the ways media "content" operates as a social currency, allowing us to form conversations with others.

Understanding fandom as an audience helps us to consider the shared meanings and pleasures that bring groups of people together around cultural products.

Learning to Read as A Fan

Today's fandoms depend on the active working through of a text that commands their attention and seems to offer depths and complexities. Here, we might understand fandom as a particular kind of audience who have found a story world that matters to them, one in which they want to collectively immerse themselves, and one that they want to decode as thoroughly and creatively as possible. They do not just watch television; they are selective and seek particular series. Watching television shows is the start rather than the end point of their interpretive practices. They decode television programs; they form social connections with others around what they watch; they make demands on the series they watch; they acquire knowledge about their production histories and discuss what authors have to say.

In *Enterprising Women: Television Fandom and the Creation of Popular Myth*, a founding work in the fandom studies tradition, Camille Bacon-Smith (1991) describes how she learned to read British genre shows such as *Blake's 7* and *The Professionals* from the perspective of a fan. A fan mentor brought VHS tapes to her house (this would have been in the late 1980s) and watched them with her, signaling which moments have been central to the fandom's relationship with the characters and story. They did not necessarily watch all the episodes in order, but rather, certain episodes or even scenes are foregrounded as part of what Bacon-Smith describes as the macroflow:

> "Much of the early ordering of the macroflow involves discerning the nature of the characters portrayed... As more material becomes available, the viewer makes a

conscious effort to fit the new episodes into the map she is building. She complains if a current episode contradicts others that preceded it. A picture builds over time to make a unified, coherent, and seemingly complete map of the series universe in the mind of the viewer... Details that reinforce the coherence of the ongoing whole may remain, while contradictory or conflicting information drops out of the meaningful structuring of the series universe" (Bacon-Smith, 1991, pp. 130-131).

She describes the social interactions that occur whenever groups of fans gather to watch episodes as particular readings of salient moments are passed along, including speculations and extrapolations that might form the basis of writing fan fiction. She also talks about what she calls "songtapes" and what are now called "vids" (see **Fandom as Desire** for fuller discussions of these practices). These fan works map the macroflow, condensing the story world into particular moments, including gestures or dialogue that seem to embody specific character relations. For this reason, the same shots may occur again and again in the vids produced within a particular fandom or lines get quoted repeatedly in fan fiction as the writer seeks to embed their new material into an already established story world. Here, we see the social dimensions of meaning-making that render a fandom a distinctive kind of audience. Bacon-Smith captures the moment where fanship gives way to fandom.

Henry recalls early conversations with his mentor John Fiske where Fiske insisted that fans differed from other readers by degree, intensifying the emotional connection and expanding and elaborating on their understanding of a fan object. However, Henry argued that fans differed in kind; that is, the genres of writing and reading that shape fandom are not the same as those driving unaffiliated audience members. The social context of group viewing—the ongoing process of interpretation and speculation on a discussion board—redefines the viewer's priorities and shapes their responses to fit into the dominant norms of the fan community. Fans may have intense debates around local particulars, but they do so within the framework of a shared consensus about what matters.

In his book *Reading in a Participatory Culture*, Henry (Jenkins et al., 2013) broke down what elements of a text became the site for fan contestation and creativity based on a lifetime of reading fan fiction. As he explains, "Fans are searching for potentials in the story which might provide a springboard for their own creative activities" (p. 141). He identifies five different elements that might provide such a grounding for a story (and which still need more klooking):

- *Kernels*: Pieces of information introduced into the narrative to hint at a larger world but not fully developed in the story itself;

- *Holes*: Plot elements readers perceive as missing from the narrative but central to their understanding of its characters;

- *Contradictions*: Two or more elements in the narrative (intentionally or unintentionally) suggesting alternative possibilities for the characters;

- *Silences*: Elements that were systematically excluded from the narrative with ideological consequences;

- *Potentials*: projections about what might have happened beyond the borders of the narrative.

Both Bacon-Smith (1991) and Jenkins (1992) argue that fans are seeking a comprehensive mapping of the narrative that serves to demonstrate their mastery but may also be the starting point for speculation and storytelling. At the center of this world are the characters, which are parsed in terms of their relationships with each other, with fans seeking in the source material moments of peak emotional intensity and revelation—moments that help them to know what the characters are feeling. The series is understood in terms of emotional realism; that is, the characters are not necessarily drawn in realistic terms, but they are intended to provoke real feelings, and they are often comprehended as if they feel what we would feel if we were in the same situation. Elements of backstory play especially vital roles in this process. To be clear, this is not how all fans read their favorite texts. However, a specific set of acquired skills and priorities emerge from the female fan fiction writing community, which is the primary focus of both *Enterprising Women* (Bacon-Smith, 1991) and *Textual Poachers* (Jenkins, 1992).

Fandoms as Interpretive Communities

Fandom, understood as a community who has learned from each other a certain way of engaging with shared texts has much in common with what Reader Response theorist Stanley Fish (1982) described as an interpretive community. Fish is interested in how different clusters of readers respond to the text in different yet predictable ways. He argues that these communities—including fan communities—not only make meanings together and develop shared interpretations through time but also develop shared norms—rules and conventions—for making meanings. They apply similar interpretive moves to other texts that get brought into the orbit of the primary interest through acts of comparison or through identifying intertexts (related works that circle in the orbit of the primary text). Interpretations, Fish argues, constitute "community property" because they emerge from social interactions and modeling within groups of readers.

Fish takes this idea even further, arguing that a text is essentially meaningless without interpretive communities and their conventions for assigning meaning; he contributed to a moment in the evolution of theories of reading where the author is "dead" and the reader is all-powerful. However, our examples above illustrate the ways authors have reclaimed their voices in a networked community, often by forging personal relationships with their fans and making active claims about what makes their works meaningful.

These bids for interpretation may or may not be accepted by their intended audience; however, they are attempts to shape the audience's activities and responses; they are signs of a new kind of relationship between audiences and producers. The fact that fandom operates as an interpretive community is what may render it opaque and difficult to understand from the outside. Anyone interested in building fan relations will need to immerse themselves in these interpretive communities before they can respect and engage with the fan culture they represent.

Moreover, as Henry and his co-author John Tulloch (1995) demonstrate in their book, *Science Fiction Audiences: Watching Star Trek and Doctor Who*: the same series may spawn different audiences who want different things from it. Henry differentiates a female-dominant community focused on character relationships explored through writing fan fiction, a male-dominant technoculture interested in the science and technology aspects of the series as problems to be solved, and a queer audience drawn to the utopian and inclusive aspect of the series, actively lobbying for LGBTQ+ themes and characters on the series. There are clearly more groups *Science Fiction Audiences: Watching Star Trek and Doctor Who* could have considered, however. For example, in doing fieldwork around *Star Trek*, Henry fell into a real-life Klingon culture, composed mostly of men, who were drawn to warrior masculinity, allowing them to reimagine their own manhood, a group informed by the then-popular success of *Iron John* (Bly, 2004) as a self-help book and movement.

Rob spent time examining the tensions and interrelationships of *Star Trek* fans' utopian ideals, their affections for the merchandise and commercial elements of the shows as media franchises, and how they interpreted them collectively (Kozinets 2001). Fans' activities were intertwined with their interpretive community's creations of meanings, which, in turn, resonated with their personal life philosophies and social critiques. For instance, numerous fan club members in the study espoused the view that *Star Trek* was a realistic template for a better society that eschews discrimination and celebrates diversity and peace. On the other hand, these same fans would use *Star Trek* merchandise to express their affiliation and identity within and beyond the fan community.

Merchandise served as both a symbol of fan identity and a medium through which fans participated and expressed support for the franchise's culture. This dual role of merchandise underscores the complexity of fan culture's relationship with consumer culture. The interpretive community that developed around products and purchasing behavior became saturated with personal meanings and communal importance. Rob also explored how marketing strategies employed by *Star Trek's* promoters interacted with the fans' expectations and experiences. Marketing and merchandise were not just matters of commercialization and profit-making but also, when done respectfully and with care, were ways to sustain and nourish the fan community and its rich and growing body of interpretations. New collectibles, new costumes, and new magazines—just like new programming, these things would provide the material culture desired for fan practices such as cosplay, collecting, and convention attending, which in turn reinforced fans' communal bonds and their shared commitment to the *Star Trek* ethos.

In a discussion of Fish's influence on our understanding of fan interpretation, Jenkins writes:

One way to understand what we mean by an interpretive community would be to think about a net discussion list as a place where people exchange their views on a common topic. Initially, as a new discussion group appears, interpretive claims might diverge wildly, yet certain consensuses emerge through discussion; members coalesce around points of mutual interest and avoid areas of dispute. Over time, the group agrees upon what kinds of posts are appropriate. In practice, larger online groups may bring together multiple interpretive communities with fundamentally different interests... As the tensions between competing interpretations mount, the group will splinter, creating competing groups (Jenkins, 2000, pp. 176-177).

We might describe these different fan communities as operating within what Tony Bennett (1983) called "reading formations." Bennett drew a distinction between readings of canonical literature texts shaped by instructions in proper academic discourses and "untutored" or "popular reading," which, he argued, the reader encounters in a less structured manner. John Tulloch (2007), for example, interviewed patrons of performances of the Russian playwright Anton Chekhov's plays, discovering a much narrower range of interpretations than he had found in his work on fan interpretations of *Doctor Who*. The Russian playwright's patrons knew what they were expected to say, and their discussions could all have been contained in a study guide for the play. Alternately, as fans encounter a work for the first time, they may, in Bennett's account, have a raw and spontaneous experience. They often do this in relation to other fan texts they have encountered and with an awareness of what constitutes meaningful elements or valid interpretive moves within the norms of their fandom.

Reading for Genre

Peter J. Rabinowitz (1985) has studied the role that genre expectations play in the reading of popular fiction, suggesting that the same work may evoke multiple genres and that what we do with the text depends on which genre becomes our starting point. For Rabinowitz, genres are "bundles of operations which readers perform in order to recover the meanings of texts rather than as sets of features found in the texts themselves... Genres can be viewed as strategies that readers use to process texts" (p. 419).

Rabinowitz discusses four different kinds of reading conventions:

1. Rules of Notice, which determine which details matter;

2. Rules of signification, which determine what things mean;

3. Rules of configuration that allow us to form expectations about the plot and

4. Rules of coherence that allow us to determine the plausibility of particular events or outcomes.

In a case study of the controversy that would disrupt the American fandom of the 1980s cult show *Beauty and the Beast*, Henry (Jenkins, 1992) deployed Rabinowitz to show the contradiction between the ways female fans read the series as a "fairy tale" romance and the ways that the producers sought to reposition it as an action series for male spectators. In a controversial effort to "retool" the series to avoid cancellation, the producers effectively reduced the female viewers who had been its original and most hardcore market into surplus viewers as they sought to recenter the series around a male viewership. This shift failed to gain traction. Henry showed how a consensus reading of the series took shape through fan writing (both fiction and nonfiction) and how the community splintered around their reactions to the genre shifts they saw taking place in the series. Henry's chapter offers a study of how a fandom's relationship with its object shifts over time in response to changes in the production process and reception context, as well as how the consensus within the community may shatter as some fans embrace the "retooled" series while others reject the changes. *Beauty and the Beast* went from a fairy tale romance to an action-adventure series where revenge was the primary motive for Vincent, the "beast," after the brutal murder of his romantic interest, Catherine. Some female fans still read it as a fairy tale romance, albeit a disappointing one, and sought signs to confirm that reading. Others felt increasingly alienated by a frustrating new genre configuration.

Fans also develop distinctive genres that they use to read texts and rewrite them. For example, we might see slash or Boy's Love (BL) as genres that emerge from the audience and can be applied to a broad range of different texts regardless of whether they are science fiction, fantasy, cop shows, detective mysteries, or westerns. Fans learn to look for particular signs that suggest that the characters might have hidden but intense feelings toward each other, and, in particular, they look for specific narrative structures. For example, what fans call "hurt comfort" (scenes where a character nurses a hurt partner) recurs across many plots and fits within the existing interpretive processes associated with the female fan fiction writing community.

Readers start to form such expectations before they engage with the fan object based on discussions with friends, say, who suggest they might like a particular work. But they also encounter movie posters, book covers, and advertising that signals what kind of work we are about to read (such paratexts were central to Bennett's approach to James Bond). From there, the vocabulary of reading strategies starts to be adjusted to the kind of text we think we are reading. Rabinowitz suggests that in the case of popular reading, such strategies are implicit and absorbed through everyday practice rather than fully articulated and formally taught. However, in fandom, mentorship of new fans is often gladly taken on by those who are passionate about particular works. Fandom has developed shared ideas about the best place for new fans to start when confronting a series they may or may not embrace as a fan object.

These kinds of theories of readership emerged at the same time that cultural studies were mapping "encoding and decoding" and using focus groups to identify the discourses that shaped the audience's response to popular media texts. Fandom studies drew insights from both traditions. Early works like *Enterprising Women* and *Textual Poachers* spent many pages identifying how fans become part of fandoms and how they acquire the skills and knowledge that allow them to read as fans. Some of these insights provided the foundation for the work on participatory culture and learning, which we discuss in **Fandom as Participatory Culture**.

As we conclude our exploration of audience interpretive strategies, we can close with the recognition that fan communities engage with media in ways that are specific and distinctive. Fans develop unique relationships with the media products they love and often actively dissect, reinterpret, and expand upon those works. They may meticulously analyze inconsistencies, fill in narrative gaps, and recontextualize character relationships through fan fiction, fan art, and theory discussions. Fans create their own systems of meaning through practices such as "vidding," where they remix scenes and characters to tell new stories or emphasize particular emotional arcs. On social media, they collaboratively interpret and debate details, develop alternative timelines, or even suggest plot resolutions the original text left unexplored. These practices are not just about enjoyment or pleasure; they allow fans to assert a sense of ownership over the narratives, transforming and co-authoring them in ways that fit their personal and collective understanding of the material.

As we move into the next and final chapter, our focus will shift to an understanding of regulative concepts and concerns. How might these varying levels of fan engagement lead to new approaches in audience segmentation? How might misunderstandings about fan intensity and segments lead to marketing mistakes? What is missing from our understanding of audience segments that might be important for managers to grasp?

The intensity of fan engagement—whether expressed through meticulous re-readings of texts, participation in fan fiction forums, or theorizing on social media—has caused the media industry to recognize the fact that different types of fans require different kinds of engagement. Instead of a homogeneous audience, managers are faced with distinctions between fans who immerse themselves fully in a narrative universe, who dip in and out, and those in between who bridge both worlds. Recognizing the differences and their implications has profound implications for how media is created, marketed, and sustained.

We will now explore how the industry caters to these different fan segments and how a greater understanding of these differences can open the door to unprecedented opportunities for fan participation and cultural production.

CHAPTER 10:
Rethinking the Fan Audience: New Approaches to Segmentation

A udience may be one of those terms, like social media, that has so many meanings and manifestations that its usage has the potential to cloud more than it conveys. Some of the manifold meanings and manifestations of the audience may not have changed in thousands of years. Watching movies like 2024's *Gladiator II*, we can imagine that the behaviors of the audiences that gathered in the Roman Colosseum to watch gladiators do battle were not significantly different from the behaviors of AS Roma fans who gathered not so far away in Stadio Olimpico, to cheer on their heroes today. Performers and singers in ancient auditoriums probably faced audiences that had a lot in common with those that perform today.

Mom, Dad, look at me! Performing for an audience seems almost hard-wired into our psyches, with child psychologists like Jean Piaget and David Elkind (1979) theorizing that an early facet of child experience is the internal belief in what the researchers called an "imaginary audience." The imaginary audience is an internalized watcher who the child believed was deeply concerned with how they performed and ever attendant to their acts (Elkind and Bowen, 1979).

Yet technology has changed what we mean by an audience and how we treat, understand, and attempt to affect it. The printing press, radio, television, and then the Internet have brought significant change to the nature of an audience and forever altered what an audience can do. These changes mark such a dramatic difference from theater performances, sports events, concerts, conventions, and other forms of live audiences that Jim Webster's (1998) tripartite classifications of "the audience" exclude. Today, those live audiences are much rarer. From social media to online newspaper letter columns to radio call-in shows to live broadcasts and many other ways, the audience keeps talking back. From tailgating to watch parties, they gather to enjoy, learn, and build their own interpretations. They refuse to simply or exclusively be the distant listeners or spectators who merely watch and absorb.

Networked communication technology expands the capabilities of the audience even more dramatically. Along with over one thousand other persons, Rob was an audience member for a live workout on his Peloton bike led by the instructor, Alex Toussaint. Throughout the workout, which was also held with a live group of participants in Peloton's New York studio, Alex was shown on camera in the background, calling out to various participants. Using their pseudonymous Peloton names, he congratulated people on reaching 1,700 or 3,000 rides today and wished others a happy birthday. When someone was in the studio who had a hallmark workout or a birthday on that day, he pointed at them and sometimes joked with or applauded them. At one point, he mentioned one of the riders and said, "She always posts when she does a workout with me and then tags me on Instagram. I love that. Everybody, do that!"

The example of Alex Toussaint, who has over 600,000 followers on Instagram, provides a complex portrait of a new type of digitally mediated real-time audience that would have been impossible to imagine just a few years ago. Not only does the audience watch Alex lead the high-intensity spin class, but Alex also watches them collectively and individually. As he conducts the class, he has access to information about them, and, as all Peloton spin instructors do, he mentions it. Moreover, there are feedback loops among the audience that usher in additional platforms. People post about Alex on social media platforms; Alex watches what they post and comments on it, inviting more posts. The audience is watching the exercise class and participating by exercising. However, they also treat the class, the Peloton brand, and Alex Toussaint's personal brand as fan objects. The actions of the collective audience and individual audience members become integrated into the performance, and participants become the audience. As with a live sports or music performance, but very personally and in ways that utilize information and media connections, the audience is intimately involved in the performance.

In our book's final chapter, we explore several paths to thinking about fans and fandoms as audiences. We begin by affirming that not all audiences are enthusiastic or favorable and extend this thinking via conceptions of anti-fans and oppositional fandoms. Next, we turn to the topic of "superfans," a term that has gained purchase in management writing about fandom in a way that we think would profit from a considerably more critical examination. Finally, we conceptualize new ways to think about audience segmentation by incorporating subtle distinctions about types of fans and what they do. In all, the chapter provides suggestions for fan-based distinctions that question several taken-for-granted yet perhaps outmoded perspectives.

Anti-Fans and Oppositional Fandoms

In "Encoding/Decoding," Stuart Hall (1980) recognized dominant, resistant, and negotiating readings, but in practice, it has been difficult to find readers who operate totally within the dominant codes. Additionally, and for the most part, those who were most resistant to the messages of the source material chose not to watch it (or so we assumed at the time). In practice, all audiences negotiated various aspects of their audiencing experience.

Jonathan Gray (2002, 2019) has proposed a different typology of affective relationships, which includes, alongside fans, "non-fans" (who are indifferent to a given program) and "anti-fans" (who share much with Hall's resistant readers). Expanding on his earlier work, Gray discusses competitive anti-fans (as in those who boo other sports fans because they are active supporters of a rival team), those who regard the text in question as a bad object on moral or ideological grounds (seeing a show as offensive in its reliance on racist stereotypes), and those who were once dedicated fans but now feel alienated because of poor production decisions (such as killing off a favorite character). The concept of anti-fan suggests that hate may be as strong an emotion as love and that one can remain an obsessive consumer of some shows precisely because you hate them (and nothing is more bitter than a fan who has fallen out of love with their object).

Figure 10.1: Typology of Fans Using Emotional Valence

We illustrate this cleaving of the fan marketplace into fans, non-fans, and anti-fans in Figure 10.1. One common form of anti-fan engagement is what is now called "hate watching," which is defined by the Urban Dictionary as "watching a TV show or movie that you hate because you hate it" (Urban Dictionary, 2013). As Gray writes, building on this definition, "some forms of hate watching tell us both about expectations one has of the media ('because it has enough promise that they hope it gets better') and expectations others have of us as viewers ('because it is so 'important' they feel that they have to'), while other forms mix dislike and pleasure in intriguing ways ('they enjoy the adrenaline that pure revulsion can bring') (Gray, 2019, p. 35).

In a case study of the "hate-watching" of *Glee* and *Smash*, Anne Gilbert (2019, p. 67) suggests that, like fandom itself, hate-watching is defined through its collaborative and performative dimensions as "necessarily social" and as a mode of critique of dominant representations of television and its fans. Gilbert references Sarah Ahmed's comment on the social nature of affect: "Together we hate, and that hate is what makes us together" (as quoted by Gilbert, 2019, p. 68). Hate-watching is often a mode of social bonding, not unlike gossip, where we bond through making moral judgments about others. While the temptation is to read hate-watching as a prime example of oppositional or resistant reading, Gray (and Gilbert) demonstrate the complex kinds of cultural negotiations that motivate such conduct.

Anti-fans also demonstrate a specific manifestation of loyalty known as oppositional brand loyalty, which extends beyond mere preference for one brand to active opposition and often denigration of a rival brand and those who support it. Brand communities are social spaces where people build a sense of connection based on their shared interest in and identification with a particular brand. These communities, facilitated by online forums, social media groups, and in-person events, offer platforms for individuals to actively engage with the brand, its products, and each other, creating a collective sense of belonging and purpose. As we explore and develop further in **Fandom as Consumer Collective**, the members of brand communities share experiences, hold discussions, and even organize actions that contribute to the reinforcement and amplification of both positive and negative brand sentiments. In many ways, these brand communities function like fandoms.

Because some collectives of fans exhibit a group form of oppositional brand loyalty, we call them *oppositional fandoms*. The fact that some fandoms have this oppositional quality makes them intriguing and potentially important to understand as audience segments. Oppositional brand loyalty has been dismissed as mere rivalry or negativity; however, it is neither of these things. Instead, it plays a vital role in shaping and defining brand communities. The act of actively opposing and criticizing rival brands is a type of loyalty test and a social glue that delineates the boundaries of the favored brand's community, creating a sense of exclusivity and reinforcing group identity.

Oppositional fandom is built upon enthusiasm and a particular kind of passionate engagement and behavior. We can easily see how these activities extend to rival fandoms who beat each other up, arguing that their favorite property is better. The K-pop landscape is rife with intense rivalries between different fandoms, each vying for their favorite group's success and recognition. Such competition can lead to online battles, vote manipulation accusations, and even real-world protests or boycotts against rival groups or their fans. There are long-standing hate wars between Marvel and DC fans, *Star Wars* and *Star Trek* fans, and PlayStation and Xbox fans, with each insisting that their brand is superior and that anyone who does not think so must be crazy. These collective criticisms reinforce the distinct identity and values of their preferred fandoms. By actively opposing these brands and their fans, these groups strengthen their sense of belonging.

Beyoncé's devoted fanbase, often referred to as the "BeyHive," has gained notoriety for its passionate defense of the artist and sometimes aggressive online behavior toward perceived rivals or critics. This behavior often manifests as targeted harassment, cyberbullying, and the spread of negative rumors or misinformation about other singers and their fans. The BeyHive's fervent support for Beyoncé often translates into a desire to protect her image and reputation. Their devotion can lead to them actively opposing and criticizing other singers who they perceive as competition or threats to Beyoncé's dominance. This oppositional loyalty can be seen in their online attacks on other artists' social media pages, music videos, or even award show performances. The BeyHive's reputation is so notorious that Prime Video loosely used it as a model for *The Swarm,* a series about a devoted fan who travels across the country killing those who dare to take her fan object's name in vain.

Managing Anti-Fans

As phenomena, anti-fans, hate-watching, and oppositional brand loyalty underscore the multifaceted nature of audience engagement. Traditionally, audience studies have primarily focused on the positive aspects of fandom, such as fan creativity, community building, and positive activism. However, oppositional brand loyalty and "anti-fandom" (groups of anti-fans drawn together by their dislike of other fans and their fan objects) draw our attention to the role of negative affect in audience engagement. They highlight how dislike, criticism, and even animosity can powerfully foster community bonds and solidify group identities. Grey's account encompasses a broad range of emotions and behaviors that can also include no emotional connection, little to no emotions, and no behaviors. It may be crucial for scholars and managers to understand that not only are there large swatches of non-fans, but there may also be significant swarms of anti-fans.

We can envision managers leveraging the power of these oppositional fandoms in numerous ways. Managers in the marketing and entertainment industries have traditionally viewed oppositional fandoms and anti-fans as liabilities, sources of negativity to be silenced or minimized. However, a more nuanced approach reveals significant opportunities to carefully recognize their emotional volatility and strong sense of identity and belonging. The energy of oppositional fandoms is part of the brand story; it can amplify brand narratives, deepen engagement, and even generate competitive advantages. Their intense emotions—whether admiration for their chosen object or animosity toward rivals—indicate a level of commitment that far surpasses mere interest.

The key lies in understanding the contexts, structures, meanings, and practices of these fandoms. For example, rivalries between fan groups, such as Marvel versus DC enthusiasts or between divergent K-pop fandoms create situations where a healthy competitive spirit can drive participation in campaigns, events, or voting contests. When channeled ethically and with integrity, these rivalries can lead to "proxy promotions" that generate significant visibility and discourse around the brand, much like long-running sports rivalries (the Chicago Bears vs. the Green Bay Packers or the New York Yankees vs. the Mets, or AC Milan vs. Internazionale Milan, for example) fuel broader interest in specific games, leagues, and teams.

By aligning oppositional fandoms with brand goals, managers can help promote a sense of inclusivity while still respecting their adversarial nature and the powerful conflicts at their core. Doing so will require the provision of platforms for creative expression, fan-driven content, and constructive dialogue. Simultaneously, managers must navigate ethical considerations to constantly defuse tensions, provide strong guidelines for correct behavior, and prevent escalation into harmful behaviors such as cyberbullying or harassment. By framing rivalries as ludic, in-control, and just-for-fun rather than high-stakes, unsupervised, and potentially destructive, brands can transform oppositional energy into a source of fan empowerment and engagement, illustrating how even negative effects can play a role in shaping consumer culture and brand loyalty.

Superfans

Segmenting a fan audience can be taken to extremes. Business-people like to talk about how the Pareto rule applies to marketing. The Pareto rule, also known as the 80/20 rule, states that roughly 80% of effects come from 20% of causes. In relation to fan segmentation, this means a small portion of a property's fanbase (about 20% of them) will likely generate the vast majority (80%) of engagement, content creation, advocacy, and revenue. Many entertainment marketers will claim that the proportions are much smaller, such that just 1 or 2% of their fans, the so-called "superfans," will drive a significant amount of revenue by, for example, buying merchandise, going to live events, or subscribing to paid channels. These superfans are often considered the most dedicated and public-facing fans. A key task of fan marketers then becomes identifying and converting these so-called superfans.

In an interview, fan scholar Daniel Cavicchi notes that the use of the term superfan has become ubiquitous over the past decade or so (Baym, Cavicchi, and Coates, 2018, p. 142). Although prior categorizations included terms such as casual fans and extreme fans, these distinctions arose as a way for members of fandoms to sort and debate fellow members' knowledge and commitment. However, Cavicchi finds that, in an age of social media, the term superfan is now used simply to describe what was previously just called a "fan"— an enthusiastic follower of a media property. The various levels of interest and passionate engagement of fans are always up for debate by fans. Still, these debates tend to be of interest mainly to members of the fandom rather than to those outside of the fandom. This is not so with the concept of superfandom, however, which has become something of a holy grail to marketers of many stripes.

In his book *Superfans: The Easy Way to Stand Out, Grow Your Tribe, and Build a Successful Business*, podcaster and entrepreneur Pat Flynn (2019) asserts that every business can create energized superfans who rival the devotees of musicians, sports teams, and celebrities. These highly engaged customers will "buy anything and everything" related to their favorite franchise (p. 18). Visualizing superfans on the top of a customer engagement pyramid, Flynn says that a sure-fire way to create lasting wealth is to create a tribe of superfans by helping them migrate from casual to active, active to connected, and then connected to superfans. The concept of superfans is based on an alleged hierarchy of fan commitment and devotion based, just as Flynn says, on the ostensible willingness of the superfan to purchase almost anything related to the fan object uncritically. This is clearly a case of audience segmentation and targeting in which uncritical willingness to pay places the superfan at the top of a segmentation hierarchy as the most desirable audience member to target.

In an interview, fan scholar Nancy Baym argues for the existence of superfans in music in a way that sounds very similar to Pat Flynn, as a type of internal competition for devotional supremacy between fans in a fandom. "There have always been 'superfans,'" she says, and this relates to "fan hierarchies and how some [fans] viewed their own [fanship] as bigger, better, and perhaps more valid than other people's fandom" (Baym, Cavicchi and Coates, 2018, p. 143). She also correlates the idea of superfans directly to "new challenges in making money from fans," viewing superfans as those who should rightfully be targeted because they are "eager to buy" physical products because they are "material manifestations of their fandom. In a digital era, autographs, posters, and handwritten lyric sheets emerge as more valuable than ever" (ibid). We discuss materiality and its relationship to fan collecting behaviors in **Fandom as Consumer Collective**. Besides building an audience, Baym sees catering to superfans as key to contemporary musicians' money-making efforts.

Passion Beyond Purchase

Baym's points are clarifying, and we agree that the superfan concept most commonly tends to be used in relation to the marketing of physical merchandise and collectibles to fans (see **Fandom as Consumer Collective** for a deeper treatment). Superfans are considered superconsumers. However, we believe that the superfan terminology does both fans and researchers a disservice. There are, for instance, several ways that fans demonstrate their devotion in ways that transcend monetary transactions, going to live events, or purchasing expensive merchandise. Yet, they engage in acts of support that have significant implications for the visibility and success of their fan objects. For example, in the K-pop community, fans organize collective efforts to stream songs repeatedly, boosting rankings on music charts and increasing their idols' visibility without directly purchasing physical products. Similarly, many different types of fans will eagerly engage in online voting contests, letter-writing campaigns, or petitions to influence outcomes in their fan object or idols' favor, such as securing awards, ensuring series renewals, advocating for trades or acquisitions, or encouraging sponsorship deals. These forms of engagement not only amplify the reach and influence of the fan object but also indirectly generate monetary value for companies through increased media exposure and brand partnerships. Beyond these measurable impacts, fans from various backgrounds also promote their idols within broader communities, becoming passionate advocates who expand their idols' reach and cultural significance. In doing so, they further entrench their idols into the popular culture zeitgeist.

Similarly, fandom is not necessarily a competitive space, and the majority of fandoms do not rank their members. There is often a recognition by fan groups that different fans may participate in a range of different ways, and fans who have not yet contributed to the life of fandom have the potential to make valuable contributions down the line. Furthermore, we find it highly questionable whether these alleged superfans (1) actually exist at all, (2) are identifiable as target markets, and (3) are as enthusiastic and uncritical purchasers as marketers and writers like Pat Flynn allege.

Mythologies of Superfans

Comparable to rumors of Bigfoot, the existence of highly uncritical fans who purchase almost anything related to their fan object might be widely believed but has never actually been seen, studied, or proven in any rigorous or reliable manner. They may exist, or they may not; we just do not know. We do not know, for instance, what percentage of an audience is composed of these superfans. We do not know how much merchandise and other material a superfan will purchase per year. We do not know if they go into debt to maintain their purchase habits. We also do not know if this alleged behavior is long-lasting or temporary. Is it a character trait, like hoarding, or a mental illness, like obsessive-compulsive disorder?

The 2024 documentary series *Selling Superman* examines the story of Darren Watts and his family. Central to the story is Darren's father, Dale Watts, an attorney from Franklin, Michigan, whose extensive collection (over 300,000 comic books) included a 1939 *Superman* #1 valued at over $3.5 million and profoundly impacted the family's dynamics. Dale's intense focus on amassing his gigantic comic book collection contributed to his divorce and resulted in emotional distance from his sons, Darren and Adam. The documentary suggests that Dale's behavior was influenced by his autism spectrum disorder, highlighting how certain mental health conditions can manifest in obsessive collecting behaviors. Should we consider Dale, who was a social isolate even from his own family, a "superfan," someone with mental illness who also happened to be a fan and collector, or something else?

Segmentation relies on more than simple labels. Who exactly are the superfans for a given franchise, and how does one identify and count them? Are there certain demographic, psychographic, geographic, or behavioral indicators that marketers should look out for? Can it possibly be sufficient to define a superfan as someone whose behavior is to purchase "anything and everything" produced related to their fan object? Even though it may be widely accepted, isn't this definition a rather ridiculous tautology or redundancy?

The notion of a fan who blindly consumes everything associated with their fan object is more a caricature than a reality. Highly engaged fans—those who invest significant amounts of time, energy, and passion into understanding the fine details of their beloved texts or products—are, by necessity, profoundly critical and discerning. Their engagement originates not from a position of mindless or passive acceptance but from an active and evaluative relationship with the object of their fandom. These fans scrutinize matters of narrative canon, production quality, authenticity, and brand consistency with an intensity that rivals that of professional critics. Paradoxically, their loyalty often hinges on this very criticality; they hold creators and producers to higher standards precisely because of their emotional investment. Rather than blindly consuming everything in sight, they carefully curate their purchases and align their evaluations of current offerings with their perceptions of what the fan object "should" be, creating a feedback loop where brands are pressured to maintain or enhance quality to meet these expectations.

Given this discerning dynamic, it seems absurd to suggest that super-fans are unthinking automatons. These are marketing fantasies—and to us, they resemble fan relation nightmares.

Mindless Consumers or Disdainful Managers?

Rob here. I remember many years ago taking my Kellogg School of Business entertainment marketing students on a field trip to the beautiful Paramount Studios in Los Angeles. After a tour of the facil-ities, the class was seated in an auditorium, and several Paramount managers gave short presentations and asked questions. One of the managers held up a bottle of water with a Star Trek label printed on it. The manager told the MBA students that it was an example of a new licensed product they would soon be releasing. I asked the manager what the link was between the bottled water and the Star Trek universe. The manager simply laughed and said, "Oh, those Star Trek fans will buy anything."

There it was, I thought. The superfan attitude. That strange, unfounded belief that they will buy anything. Although I bit my tongue so as not to offend our hosts, I left that tour with a sour taste in my mouth, believing that the managers' attitude was dis-dainful and disrespectful toward the fan base that had supported the franchise for decades. More than this, I felt that the managers were role-modeling the wrong message to the students. It was not until much later, following the discussions of the superfan concept in class with Henry, that I was better able to fully articulate the endemic problems with the insulting superfan idea.

Both here. We acknowledge that there are fans who purchase a lot of merchandise or services. But can we really say it is an "over-pur-chase"? The distinction between wants and needs is crucial. You might believe that you have a deep need for a coffee in the morning, perhaps a certain kind like a mocha frappuccino. To us, your request looks like a want rather than a need. But who are <u>we</u> to say what <u>you</u> need or want? Academics calling themselves critical, neo-Marxist, or cultural critics have been making these distinctions for a long time, judging others' consumption as based on either want versus need or necessity versus luxury. But we live in a world where much of our consumption would be considered very luxurious compared to what our ancestors of only a few generations prior would say they needed.

As well, our understanding of the reasons behind these behaviors is very different from the managers who simply say they will purchase anything offered to them. It is not because they are mindless drones who subserviently bow to anything offered to them just because they are "superfans." It is because they find benefit in the purchase, event, or gathering. Assuming away any critical faculty on the part of these fans is not just bad manners; it can end up being bad business. The trash heaps of industry are littered with companies that took for granted that their customers so adored them that their loyalty was assured. Toys R Us, MySpace, Kodak, and Radio Shack had customers who loved them—until they didn't. However, once the companies stopped offering what those customers wanted, the love affair ended.

Some of the people who call themselves "superfans" may well be involved in fanships rather than members of fandoms (Amesley, 1989). They may be those, like Superman #1 super-collector Dale Watts, who are least connected to larger fan communities and thus who operate outside its more cooperative and collaborative norms. It is certainly possible, even likely, that there are some fans who enjoy maintaining nearly complete collections of particular types of products. Call them devoted collectors, committed consumers, or avid accumulators, but please do not reduce them to stereotypical caricatures. Segmentation is all about finding groups with similar characteristics and marketing to their needs. Much of the time it might involve aggregating the needs of many people and serving that group. It certainly is not intended to be used to locate specifically vulnerable individuals and prey on them. For our purposes, we see more potential in learning about the main types of fan groups, figuring out what they want, and understanding them as thinking and discerning individuals.

Contextualizing Audience Analysis

Thinking about fanships and fandoms as audiences should encourage us to rethink how we recognize, investigate, and work with fans and fandoms. Traditionally, media audience analysis grew up in a world of big newspapers and two or three major television channels per country. Under those media-constrained conditions, using broad categorizations such as the audience-as-mass viewpoint could capture important aspects of the audience experience. Today, however, there is an overemphasis on amassed ratings, subscriber numbers, reach, and impressions, which risks overlooking the high-octane and multi-dimensional nature of fandoms. In a digital and multifaceted media environment, there is a hunger and growing recognition that a more contextualized approach to audience segmentation is necessary—one that does not split the audience world into nonfans and superfans but, instead, acknowledges the spectrums of fan participation.

Traditional segmentation schemes like the Hollywood quartiles often limit us to static categories like age, gender, or geographical location, which can reveal very little about who fans or fandoms are and what drives them. A story told in John Schouten and Jim McAlexander's (1995) research on subcultures of consumption expresses this idea perfectly. The authors relate the case of a boyhood friend of one of the authors. Chuck, whose given name was Carlos, was born to Mexican parents in Los Angeles. Chuck grew up in a diverse neighborhood and understood Spanish, although he refused to speak it. By traditional markers, he would be categorized as a "young Hispanic male," with assumptions about his values and consumption patterns aligning with that identity (p. 59). However, anyone who knew Chuck knew this was not the case. His prized possession was a surfboard, which he carried on a compact pickup truck equipped with surfboard racks. His wardrobe reflected a quintessential "surfer" style, and his closest friends—all surfers—never heard him speak Spanish. Chuck eventually married a blonde "surfer chick," reinforcing his identity within a surfing subculture rather than the sociological category assigned to him by the U.S. Census (ibid). Chuck's identity exemplifies how, in consumer culture, people define themselves not by demographic labels but by the activities, objects, and relationships that imbue their lives with meaning.

We develop and discuss Schouten and McAlexander's important notion of subcultures in the **Fandom as Consumer Collective** and **Fandom as Subculture** books. For our purposes in this book about audiences, the key point is that the self-identification of a member of a fandom is often much stronger than the imposed sociological constructs that census makers or marketers assign to them. That strong self-identification as a fan may be interrelated with many things about that person's behaviors, including things like where they live, what they do for a living, what car they drive, what they do on the weekends, who they hang around with, and even who they marry. Far beyond mere acts of audiencing, these leisure pursuits are passionate engagements that can have major implications in people's lives.

Nine Types of Fans Audience: Reconsidering Traditional Fan Segmentation

Demographics and psychographics are still widely used in marketing, entertainment marketing, and fandom relations. However, there is significant potential to develop behavioral segmentation and direct behavioral targeting in these areas better. Although its accuracy depends on how it is applied, behavioral segmentation has the benefit of classifying people by what they do rather than ascribing behaviors to them based on some category, such as assuming Chuck will vote or purchase like other young Latinos because he fits into this category. Further, we think that a helpful starting point for fan segmentation can be found in the fanship-fandom continuum we develop in **Defining Fandom**.

For convenience and tractability, the Fanship-Fandom Continuum breaks down fanship and fandom behaviors into six behavioral responses: (1) enjoying the fan object, (2) discussing that enjoyment with family and friends, (3) searching for and reading online information about the fan object, (4) attending a live fan object-based event, (5) regularly posting about the fan object, and (6) creating and sharing creative works based on the fan object with other fans. There are three other attitudes or behaviors that we can use and develop based on some of the categories we have discussed in this chapter. First are the non-fans who are unattached to, uninterested in, or unaware of crossing over. Next are anti-fans who passionately resist fan objects and fandoms. Last are the highly discerning and acquisitive devoted fan collectors, who are not to be considered mindless superfans.

The nine types of fan audiences are as follows: non-fans, anti-fans, enjoyers, discussers, searchers, posters, attenders, creators, and collectors. Beyond these nine categories, additional contextualizing can be done. For example, there are also audience members who are in the audience because of other people rather than because of their own volition. Consider the partner who watches the romantic comedy because their beloved wants to see it with them or the beleaguered friend who is uninterested in cricket but goes along to be a good companion. There might be those who audience something for work or because it was assigned to them. There can also be non-human audiences. All of these possibilities can be interesting to investigate. However, as a starting point, we will consider the behaviors of these nine different types of fan audiences and explore how they could lead to new perspectives on entertainment and fan marketing.

How are these nine types different from the demographic quadrants we illustrated earlier in this book as an important segmentation tool still employed in Hollywood decision-making? These nine fanship and fandom-based types are not necessarily mutually exclusive. Non-fans can also be anti-fans. In fact, the behaviors of later types may well be embedded in those of the early types, and behavioral elements like discussing, posting, and creating often might overlap. We would expect many of these types to also enjoy the fan object and for creators to participate as posters. However, there are also clear boundaries encouraging us to see the distinctness of individual fans' fanships and fandoms. Creators may or may not be attendees, and some may not be discussers. The reality is (as reality often is) complicated, which is why attending to actual fan behaviors in real-world contexts can be so rewarding. Now, consider the following descriptions of these types of the overall audience.

- *Non-fans:* A type of non-audience characterized by their indifference toward specific cultural texts, media properties, or brands. Unlike fans or anti-fans, who engage actively with fan objects—whether positively or negatively—non-fans are generally disengaged, neither consuming nor critiquing the content in question. Their detachment offers marketers and scholars a baseline for understanding audience segments that do not actively participate in fan culture. Non-fans are valuable for comparative studies, highlighting the boundaries and defining characteristics of fandoms. For ambitious marketers, they may offer an entry point as well.

- *Anti-fans:* An audience type that engages with media or brands they actively dislike or oppose. Unlike non-fans, their engagement is driven by a critical stance, often manifested through practices like hate-watching, critique, or active opposition.

Anti-fans can be motivated by ideological disagreements, moral objections, or dissatisfaction with creative decisions, as seen with alienated fans of franchises like Star Wars. This segment also includes oppositional brand loyalty, where negative sentiment toward one brand reinforces allegiance to its competitors, such as Manchester United vs. Manchester City or Marvel vs. DC. For marketers, these groups present challenges and opportunities, as their behaviors influence public discourse and shape perceptions of cultural and commercial products. Recognizing their impact offers deeper insights into the multifaceted nature of audience engagement.

- *Enjoyers*: An audience type composed of those who repeatedly audience the fan object. These fans are likely to be relatively solitary in their enjoyment and engagement with the fan objects. Their fanship is lower commitment, convenience-oriented, and inconsistent, and they tend to avoid deep dives into lore, trivia, background material, or specialized fan content. They might be interested in premium access to their primary fan object, standalone experiences, or perhaps basic fan apps. They are not seeking intensive community participation or overly specialized offerings.

- *Discussers:* An audience type who discuss or share their fan objects with friends, family, and coworkers but who do not participate in larger fan communities, fan conventions, or online discussions or create fan works. This group may be interested in information about their fan object and might occasionally visit websites that provide such information. Discussers might find tidbits of information relevant to share with others in their immediate social environment. They might wear affiliated clothing like a jersey or concert t-shirt and might appreciate gifts based on it. Marketers might try attracting discussers to some ancillary goods and services like playlists, entry-level fan content such as behind-the-scenes videos, and interactive one-off, pop-up, or movie/television events.

- *Searchers:* This audience type regularly searches for and digests online information and social media posts about the fan object. Although not engaged in any connective behavior beyond regular searching and reading, they will likely come across information about fan collectives. They may want to begin posting as well, which will move them into the poster type. Perspicacious managers relating to the searcher type will be keen to ascertain their interests, goals, tendencies, and the types of material to which they are responding.

- *Posters:* This audience type contains people who are regularly engaged in posting about fan objects on social media. We consider this activity to be a contribution to the online collective of other people passionately engaged with the fan object. By regularly sharing information and their viewpoints, this type of fan is establishing a connective and collective relationship with both the fan object and other fans, putting them on the verge of, if not already within, the realm of fandom. More penetrant analysis would try to determine the motivations, inclinations, and specific fascinations of the members of this type who are of interest to marketers.

- *Attenders:* This type of audience has attended a live fan object-based event, which could be in person or virtual (which may be a different type of attendance). By attending an event such as a concert, a sporting event, or a convention, the fan connects with others outside their immediate social network and is also exposed to the broader world of fandom, with its shared interests and desires. Consider the mix of powerful emotions of someone who has been a lifelong Marvel fan going to Comic-Con for the first time or a devoted BLACK-PINK fan at their first concert. Treated as a market segment, marketers could provide unique opportunities for attendees to attend, extend, and memorialize their participation.

- *Creators*: A fan who creates and shares creative works that are based on the fan object with other fans. This behavior enacts participatory culture; creators are behaving as members of a fandom. The fan creates something, whether fiction, art, music, or translated subtitles of foreign productions, that both relates to the fan object and is potentially valuable for the actual or potential members of the fandom. Rather than clouding this behavior with stereotypical descriptions, it may be useful to understand the specific kinds of behaviors that creators do and think about what sorts of tools, connections, and techniques they need to do it better. Because of what they do, the members of this segment have numerous needs related to their fan objects and fandom. Marketers might think about how to facilitate those needs in a mutually beneficial manner (and we mean mutually beneficial to fans, brands, and fandoms).

- *Collectors*: A type of fan defined by their active engagement in the acquisition and curation of items related to their fan object. Unlike caricatured notions of "superfans," collectors exhibit a discerning approach, emphasizing agency and variety in their practices. This type of fan will often focus their collecting on specific niches, such as rare merchandise, vintage memorabilia, or limited-edition releases, driven by personal taste, historical significance, or aesthetic value. Collectors also engage in knowledge-sharing within communities, contributing to the broader cultural and material narratives of fandoms. Their diverse practices balance personal passion with broader cultural participation. Marketers and researchers seeking to target collectors as customers should acknowledge and appreciate their nuanced preferences and priorities, recognizing them as influential tastemakers within their fandoms who shape demand, values, and collective fan identities.

By more deeply exploring the categories in this segmentation, marketers and media producers may be able to better tailor their approaches to different levels of fan passion and engagement, ensuring that each segment is engaged in a way that resonates with their specific locus of interest and interaction. Conducting audience segmentation in this way can help avoid the stereotyping and oversimplification that comes with a simple split between non-fans and fans (or, worse, "superfans") while keeping the segments simple enough to be useful. Fan segments drawn from these categories could certainly be used to devise managerial goals that match the standards of the SMART acronym: Specific, Measurable, Achievable, Relevant, and Time-bound. These characteristics are widely accepted as the qualities of successful objective setting.

Key Characteristic Fan Segmentation

Another approach might dimensionalize the five key characteristics attributed to members of fandom in **Defining Fandom**. Members of fandom are passionate, so how does this passion express itself? Can we measure this passion and find its dimensions? We can use helpful measurement tools like the "connectedness" scale of Russell, Norman, and Heckler (2004). Masayuki Yoshida et al. (2014) have devised and tested a fan engagement scale in sports contexts that might also be useful. Linda Hollebeek, Mark Glynn, and Roderick Brodie (2014) developed and validated a measure of consumer brand engagement in social media that is also relevant in online contexts. In other words, there are plenty of excellent tools that might help researchers, teachers, students, and managers differentiate the different types of fandom and engagement expressed and experienced by the members of their audience. However, these tools are not specifically designed to help managers understand audiences or fan audiences in particular. The tools are not very dynamic and lack dynamism—one is over 20 years old, while two are over 10 years old. They are not adapted to the rapidly changing circumstances of modern fandom, which is technologically light-years ahead of where it was just a decade ago.

Members of fandom are also connected, so can we differentiate the different ways that they are connected? Online versus offline is one such general way. However, there are temporal and spatial dimensions at play here as well. Are fans connected only temporarily, such as by sitting next to one another at an event, or is this a more regular meeting? Do they build personal bonds of affiliation where they know each other's names and birthdays, or is this a more anonymous or pseudonymous arrangement?

Members of fandoms are creative. It will help to distinguish the types of creativity they exhibit. Are they artistic or literary? Do they like genre-bending or gender-bending fiction? Do they share their creations, and if so, where and how?

Acknowledging these different characteristics and behaviors means recognizing the specific and varied ways fans interact with their passions. When members of a fandom are critical, what do they criticize and how? When they are active, what are some of their main activities, and how, when, and with whom are they pursued? Some may collect memorabilia; others may help organize and attend live events; others still might engage primarily through contributing to discussions on online platforms. Each of these types of fans has different expectations and needs, and recognizing these differences allows for more targeted and meaningful engagement strategies.

Taking inspiration from online selling platforms like Etsy, where individual creativity and niche market interests thrive, we can consider more fine-grained forms of segmentation that appreciate, acknowledge, and cater to diverse and specific consumer needs. For instance, consider the case of a fan who crafts bespoke merchandise like Henry's *Wednesday* shirt. This niche product taps into the specific tastes and interests of fans of the series both rapidly and for an affordable price. This kind of segmentation recognizes and acknowledges the unique and often granular preferences within fandoms, moving beyond generic products to provide deeply resonant offerings at near-lightning speed.

This approach to fan segmentation helps avoid the pitfalls of decontextualization. Too often, fans, like other audience members, are reduced to data points, stripped of the rich social and cultural contexts that define their fanship experiences and memberships in fandoms. Instead, a more holistic approach should involve observing and seeking to understand fans in natural social environments and gaining insights through direct engagement rather than relying solely on automated classifications or self-reported data.

The goal of this refined segmentation is not simply to sell more products; instead, it is to gain insight that can assist in building more lasting and powerful relationships between fan objects, media producers, and their audiences. By understanding and appreciating the varied and complex ways fans engage with their passions, media companies can create content and products that truly resonate across the multifarious worlds of fanship and fandom. It also may set the stage for a greater comprehension of fandom not only as a commercial phenomenon but as an important part of the social and cultural tableau, with active audience members writing and illustrating their roles in the continuously evolving narrative of media and culture.

Behavioral Targeting in Fandom's Future

Behavioral targeting represents a dramatic shift in the marketing world, one that could redefine how brands interact with fans by focusing on individual behaviors rather than traditional demographic or psychographic categories. Unlike segmentation—a practice that groups consumers together into predefined categories and assumes that the members can be treated alike—behavioral targeting leverages real-time data from myriad digital interactions, sourcing transactions such as search histories, purchase patterns, streaming habits, and even engagement with specific posts. By analyzing these behavioral markers, marketers can identify not just what a specific fan likes but what they do. This type of information can inform marketers when and how the audience member engages. It can even estimate the level of passionate commitment in particular engagements. This granular approach enables marketers, like never before, to deliver personalized content, products, and experiences that align with individual fan preferences. Although some might find this level of intimacy creepy, others will recognize it as not dissimilar to systems already in place with Amazon, Apple, Google, and other technology companies that are already interacting closely with customers.

The rise of AI amplifies the potential of behavioral targeting, making "markets of one" a feasible reality. In this paradigm, AI systems analyze vast datasets, identify patterns, and generate tailored marketing campaigns that resonate uniquely with each individual fan. For example, a sports brand could dynamically adjust its messaging to appeal to fans based on their favorite team, recent game attendance, or engagement with highlight reels. Similarly, music labels can target listeners not just by genre preference but through their most-streamed songs or favorite concert venues, much as Spotify already does, as it demonstrates with its end-of-year "Wrapped wrap-ups." Spotify is an excellent example of the shift we envision from broad levels of segmentation to hyper-personalization. As those techniques become more widespread, they will transform fan marketing by enabling brands to anticipate and respond to fans' needs with near-instantaneous precision, fostering more powerful emotional connections and more profound levels of customer loyalty.

The implications of behavioral targeting for fan marketing might reshape entertainment, sports, music, and cult branding landscapes. As we discussed earlier in this book, digital content personalization, such as Netflix's "Bandersnatch," illustrates how the choose-your-own-adventure interactivity of technologies is already redefining the world of media production and consumption. As content fragments into hyper-customized experiences, marketers increasingly transform into roles that facilitate ongoing co-creation practices rather than sell particular time or audience slots for watchers or listeners. Imagine fans of a music artist generating new songs that are indistinguishable from their older ones. Imagine Elvis Presley singing a new song such as Lady Gaga's "Hold My Hand" or Frank Sinatra singing "Defying Gravity" from *Wicked*? Custom-made songs and setlists for virtual concerts are as possible as watching historic games or impossible re-enactments, such as Babe Ruth's 1927 New York Yankees baseball team facing off against the 2024 World Series Champion Los Angeles Dodgers. Any television show, real or long in the past, can become subject to an ongoing or freshly crafted narrative arc. These productions will deepen engagement to an unprecedented level that seamlessly combines creation and consumption. They position fans as creative participants in the brand ecosystem, creating all sorts of problems for creators and copyright holders. These changes in segmentation herald a striking new world of challenges and possibilities.

As AI-driven behavioral targeting advances, its integration into fan relations and fandom brand marketing requires that managers navigate confusing labyrinths of new ethical implications. Not only will the leveraging of fan data and respecting fans' privacy be a delicate and ongoing balancing act—just as it already is—but more so. Not only will licensing and rights be increasingly threatened and renegotiated, but as fandoms embrace co-creation, marketers will be challenged to keep up with the constant reconfiguration of a mass cultural and popular cultural panorama that threatens to disintegrate into an isolated world of interwoven individualistic impulses, onanistic fantasies, and personal brand loyalties—a likely outcome of the gravitational pull of fragmenting entertainment into 8 billion "markets of one." Oh, brave new world of segmentation and behavioral targeting that has such choices in it! The future of audiences is going to be wilder and weirder than ever.

Wrapping Up

This book has led you through a detailed landscape of ideas considering fans and fandoms as complex audiences. This chapter has aimed to dissect and expand upon traditional notions of audience segmentation, pushing beyond mere labels like "superfans" to explore the multifaceted behaviors through which fanship and fandom membership manifest. We delved into the nuances of oppositional fandoms and anti-fans and emphasized the different ways audiences engage with, critique, and even resist. By introducing more dynamic and nuanced segmentation strategies, we hope to encourage approaches that respect the varied expressions of fandom and enrich our understanding of how these diverse engagements contribute to the broader media landscape. Moving forward, we encourage researchers, students, and practitioners alike to test and work with these refined segmentation methods while also ensuring that they remain sensitive to the cultural and contextual factors that influence fan behavior. By reimagining how we conceptualize and interact with fandom as an audience, we pave the way for a more inclusive and participatory future in media studies, audience research, and media and marketing management.

Exercise: Mapping Your Fan Communities

Let's start from the premise that being an audience is a shared social practice. You can audience any kind of audio, visual, or audiovisual content. It can be something that you stream, listen to on the radio, read, or watch on your computer screen or even on your phone. It could include watching YouTube videos or even TikTok videos or Instagram stories. But you may also want to just focus on the programming you watch on a big screen in the presence of other people.

In the first step, try to map some of the sports, shows, or others you watch most often and identify who you watch them with (if anyone), who you discuss them with, who recommended them to you, and who you have suggested them to. Let's consider this the immediate social circle that helps shape your viewing of these programs.

Now, focus on one particular media production. Who do you think is the audience for this type of production? How would you describe them? Do any of the audience classification types in this book resonate with you?

Are all the members of this "imagined audience" for this program people like you? Are they different from you? How do you think the producers of this production thought about who the audience would be? Why do you think that? What are some of the cues or clues to who producers thought they would reach or wanted to reach?

Next, think about what you do with this programming. Other than receiving it in front of some sort of screen, how does it activate you if it does? If it does activate you in some way—to discuss it, to write something, to go online, to draw, post, or write—then please describe or even share that.

For our second-to-last step, focus on people you know only online, the critics or podcasters whose opinions you take seriously, the discussion boards you visit, and other online spaces that shape your relationship with each program.

Try drawing a picture to represent those relationships. You can map them in whatever way you want, but you want to try to convey as much of the information above as possible.

Look at what you have produced about your own audiencing of one piece of media programming. How might we contrast these findings with the idea of the television watcher as an isolated, autonomous viewer, which so often informs industry discourse?

GLOSSARY

Agency: The capacity of individuals and groups to act upon and construct their identities within a world not of their own making, sometimes described as structure.

Appropriation: the act of taking cultural resources and deploying them towards your own ends, often involving fans reworking popular narratives.

Appointment television: Television that you have to reschedule your life to be sure to watch because it is only aired at a particular time slot.

Attenders: Proposed fan target market segment referring to a segment of fans that have attended a live fan object-based event of some kind.

Audience: The group of people who engage with, consume, or are targeted by a specific piece of media, event, or marketing campaign. This group can be defined broadly (e.g., the audience of a national television network) or narrowly (e.g., viewers of a specific YouTube channel).

Audience-as-Mass: An audience research perspective that conceives of an audience as a large, undifferentiated group of people who receive media messages or marketing campaigns; a view rooted in earlier media effects theories that examined mass media like radio and television and considered the audience to be a passive receiver of messages, largely homogeneous and similarly influenced by the content they consume.

Audience-as-Outcome: An audience research perspective that conceives of an audience by the effects or impacts that media or marketing efforts have on them; a view focused on measuring how effectively a message achieves its intended impact.

Audience-as-Agent: An audience research perspective that conceives of an audience as participants who interpret, reinterpret, or contest the media they consume based on their own cultural backgrounds, experiences, and social contexts; an approach that acknowledges the audience's power to shape the meaning of media texts, to create or spread fan content, and to influence media production through their actions and feedback.

Audiencing: The shared set of activities and stances constituting the dynamic process by which a person or persons audience, consume, engage with, and are affected and inspired by media productions and their distribution; the concept includes various ways that people engage with media productions.

Blank Slate Characters: characters in the source text that are underdeveloped, allowing or requiring the fan fiction writer to develop them from scratch.

Classical Hollywood Cinema: A mode of cinematic production defined by cause-event structures, a strong sense of closure, use of continuity editing and other devices to ensure clear spectator orientation, etc.

Coalition Audience: The audience is made up of groups with different interests, and the program is structured to provoke discussion or otherwise serve the needs of each.

Collective Intelligence: The capacity of participants within a networked culture to pool and work through information together to arrive at a conclusion that would be impossible for individuals to achieve on their own.

Contradictions: One of the prompts for fan fiction writing refers to cases where there is a lack of consistency in the information provided about a particular issue.

Creators: Proposed fan target market segment referring to fans who create and share creative works based on fan objects with other fans.

Culture: The subject of a core debate in the sciences, with one side viewing it as "the best that man has created" (i.e., high culture versus low culture) and the other reading it as the total way of life for a particular community (i.e., Raymond Williams' "culture is ordinary" approach, as explained in this book).

Cultural Appropriation: Generally used today as a rebuke for taking forms of culture that do not authentically belong to your community and exploiting them for a purpose that does not serve the needs of the community that produced them.

Decoding: In Stuart Hall's communication theory context, the process by which audiences interpret and make sense of media content involves extracting meaning from the message based on the audience's own cultural background, experiences, and social context; it can result in different levels of understanding or interpretation, ranging from accepting the dominant or intended meaning, negotiating a more personalized interpretation, or outright rejection of the message based on personal or group beliefs.

Dippers: The middle segment of the audience who want to participate in an immersive entertainment experience and also actively share their discoveries with friends and family.

Discussers: A proposed fan target market segment that refers to fans who discuss or share their fan objects with friends, family, and coworkers but who do not participate in larger fan communities, fan conventions, or online discussions or create fan works.

Divers: The hardcore fans who have the most intensive relationship with the content, want to explore deeply, and often spread the content with others.

Encoding: In Stuart Hall's communication theory, context refers to the process by which media producers and communicators construct messages, integrating culturally and ideologically informed meanings into media content; it involves selecting specific signs, symbols, and language that convey the intended message within a particular technical and production framework.

Engagement television: a form of television audiences actively seek out, can be watched at any time for any purpose.

Enjoyers: The proposed fan target market segment refers to fans who enjoy the fan object.

Extensive vs. Intensive Reading: A form of reading where one consumes a broad range of texts and understands them in relation to each other.

Fan: People who care passionately about some sector of popular culture, who creatively and critically engage with its products, and who actively share their passions with others. These interests may or may not, as we will see, translate into more active and extensive consumption of cultural products, from media franchises to consumer brands.

Fandom Studies: The examination of the social, cultural, economic, and political lives of a particular kind of passionate public—groups of people who are engaged with some form of popular culture (a television series, a film, a comic book, a game, a sports team, a pop performer or rock group, or so much more). Often, the entertainment industry conceives of fans as individual audience members who have shown some interest in a specific property or fan object. There are some academics who also study individual fans; however, for the most part, fandom studies are interested in collective rather than individual behavior, whether in the family unit, the workplace, or some larger subcultural community.

Fanboy Auteur: A rhetorical strategy where television figures claim allegiance with the fans against the "powers that be" and use this rhetoric to claim authenticity for the works they produce.

Fanship: The affective relationship that any individual fan may have with a cultural product.

Fandom: The social structures with which fans affiliate with each other for the purpose of sharing their passions and interests. Fans may or may not join an organized fandom; however, the majority of people belong to some larger "community"—a family unit, a group of co-workers or dorm-mates, etc.—within which they discuss what they like and what they mean to them.

Forensic Fandom: The group of people who seek out problems and mysteries to solve in the text and who work through them together as online social networks.

Hate-watching: A mode of viewer engagement where fans (or antifans) may take pleasure in making fun of those elements that might otherwise frustrate them about the series.

Holes: Gaps in the information a narrative provides, which fans might seek to fill with their own speculations

Hunters and Gatherers: A group that responds to the dispersed nature of the transmedia texts by seeking out and sharing bits and pieces of media content with others in their network

Imaginary Communities: The sense of connection we have to a community even though we may never know all of the people within it

Imagined Audiences: The audience that the creator of a work has in mind, often an idealized sense of who the fans, viewers, or consumers are.

Intensive Reading: A form of reading where one engages with a few texts, reading them over and over again for deeper understanding.

Interpretive Community: A group that collectively assigns meaning and develops shared interpretations, even rules of interpretation, together

Intersectionality: The ways that an individual may belong to multiple kinds of identities that offer differing degrees of power and privilege.

Intervention Analysis: A mode of ethnographic audience research that seeks to amplify and mobilize the voices of those who feel excluded from positions of power within the entertainment industry

Kayfabe: The presenting of staged events in professional wrestling as if they were real, a set of conventions increasingly shared between performers and audiences that historically separated out those in the know from marks or rubes.

Kernels: Small bits of information that might serve as inspiration or a building block for fan fiction.

Media Producer-Fan Audience Production Loop: This concept describes the cyclical interaction between media producers and fan audiences, where content creation and consumption are intertwined; media producers encode cultural meanings into their works, which are then decoded by fan audiences; fans, in turn, actively respond to these messages by creating their own content—including such things as podcasts, posts, creative works, signs, costumes, or commentary—that feeds back into the production process; it emphasizes the active role of fans not just as consumers but as participants in an ongoing process of expanding fan object-related media production, influencing future content and reshaping the cultural discourse; the loop highlights the dialogic nature of modern media communication, where production and reception are part of an ongoing, iterative process.

Microaggression: A statement or act that is experienced as demeaning for someone in a marginalized group, even if it was not fully intentional, a localized exercise of power and privilege.

Migratory Audiences: A group that moves from one media franchise to another when the producers no longer satisfy their needs and desires

Networked Audiences: The form of social community that emerges amongst audience members as they begin to exploit the properties of networked communication

Oppositional Fandom: A collective of fans who actively define their loyalty to a brand, artist, or property by opposing and criticizing rival brands or fan groups; the behavior is not merely about rivalry or negativity but serves as a key element in strengthening the identity and boundaries of the fan community.

Potentials: A possibility hinted at but not fully developed in the source material that could be a springboard for fan fiction

Quadrants: A common Hollywood segmentation technique involving splitting the general movie-going audience into male and female and over and under the age of twenty-five; also inaccurately termed "quartiles," the technique is a crude demographic attempt to consider a wider variety of tastes (than, presumably, the tastes of the filmmakers themselves).

Queer Baiting: Hints of same-sex desire within popular fiction (or by people associated with the production) that are read by fans as a promise for fuller development of the relationship, usually used under circumstances where the promise goes unfulfilled.

Posters: Proposed fan target market segment referring to a segment of fans regularly engaged in posting about the fan object on social media.

Powerless Elite: A term used to describe the contradictory experience of being a fan who sees themself as part of an elite because of their superior knowledge and intense development of the property but who lacks the access and authority to protect those elements in the series to which they feel so invested.

Racebending: A term that has been used to refer to the transformation of the race of a character, whether as a critique of industry practices of recasting characters of color with White actors or the fan practice of imagining presumed White characters as people of color.

Reading Formations: The protocols for reading, interpretation, and use that emerge from an interpretive community

Reception vs. Reproduction: In the "encoding and decoding model," reception refers to the moment of decoding and immediate interpretation, and reproduction refers to the various ways that fans and other audiences make use of the media content they decipher.

Searchers: The proposed fan target market segment refers to a segment of fans who regularly search for and read online information and social media posts about the fan object.

Segmentation: The process of taking a multifaceted mass market and dividing it into smaller subgroups that are more similar within themselves than they are between one another; members assigned to these "homogeneous" subgroups will allegedly display similarities in needs, preferences, and/or behaviors. [see also **Targeting** and **Target Audience**].

Silences: Those issues which the source material fails to address, which may become the starting point for writing fan fiction

Structure: In Giddens' theory, the recurrent social practices, rules, and resources that shape and constrain human behavior are both the medium and the outcome of social action, meaning that while they guide and influence individuals' actions, they are also created and reproduced through those actions. Structure and agency are interdependent, as individuals (agents) act within these structures but also have the capacity to change and reshape them over time.

Superfan (a fictitious stereotyped character): A highly dedicated and passionate segment of a fanbase, often representing a small percentage of the total audience; rumored to drive a disproportionate amount of revenue for a brand or property; typically considered the most loyal and vocal fans, frequently purchasing merchandise, attending live events, and subscribing to premium services; a key focus for entertainment marketers, almost like a holy grail.

Surplus Audience: An audience that was not intended but who emerges because of their active interest in another space for extending the market.

Surplus Blackness: The idea that Black audiences are regarded by the media industries as surplus audiences.

Skimmers: The segment of the audience that has a casual, disinterested, and relatively superficial relationship to the content.

Target Audience: A specific group of audience members that a media producer, business, marketer, or other type of communicator aims to reach with its products, services, or messages; often identified based on various segmentation variables such as demographic, psychographic, and behavioral factors such as age, gender, income, interests, or purchasing behavior. [See also **Segmentation**].

Targeting: The process of selecting and focusing marketing efforts on specific segments of the population that are most likely to respond positively to a media production or other product, service, or message; after identifying a target audience, businesses and marketers use targeting strategies to tailor their communications, products, and campaigns to the preferences, behaviors, and needs of that particular group. [See also **Segmentation**].

Thick Description: A mode of cultural analysis that circles around its object of study, providing layers of analysis that emerge from looking at it in different contexts or from varied perspectives.

Transmedia Authorship: A logic whereby the reader is invited to construct a mental model of the author from information and performances spread across the media landscape, which shapes how she reads and responds to any particular text.

Transmedia Storytelling: A process where integral elements of a fiction get dispersed systematically across multiple delivery channels for the purpose of creating a unified and coordinated entertainment experience. Ideally, each medium makes its own unique contribution to the unfolding of the story.

REFERENCES

Akitunde, T. (2023). *Fandom Whisperer: How Campfire creates immersive experiences that feel real.* https://blog.dropbox.com/topics/customer-stories/campfire#:~:text=Steve%20Coulson%3A%20We%20call%20it,they%27re%20the%20least%20engaged

Amesley, C. (1989). 'How to Watch Star Trek,' *Cultural Studies*, 3(3), pp. 323–339.

Reid, A. and Anderson, B. (1985). 'Imagined Communities. Reflections on the origin and spread of nationalism.' *Pacific Affairs*, 58(3), p. 497. https://doi.org/10.2307/2759245.

Arnold, M. (1869). *Culture and Anarchy.* Smith, Elder.

Associated Press, (2014). Ronald D. Moore Shares His Outlander Strategy. 14 August. Available at: https://www.youtube.com/watch?v=TApo_3Yql9A

Bacon-Smith, C. (1991). *Enterprising Women: Television Fandom and the Creation of Popular Myth.* University of Pennsylvania Press.

Barker, M. (2006). Making Middle-Earth Sound Real: The Cultural Politics of the BBC Radio Edition. In: E. Mathijs, ed. *The Lord of the Rings: Popular Culture in Global Context.* Wallflower Press, pp. 61–70.

Barker, M., Smith, C. & Attwood, F. (2023). *Watching Game of Thrones: How Audiences Engage with Dark Television.* University of Manchester Press.

Bartle, R. A. (undated). 'Hearts, Clubs, Diamonds, Spades: Players Who Suit MUDs'. Available at: https://mud.co.uk/richard/hcds.htm.

Baym, N., Cavicchi, D. & Coates, N. (2018). 'Music Fandom in the Digital Age: A Conversation'. In: *The Routledge Companion to Media Fandom.* Routledge, pp. 141–152.

Bennett, A. (2015). 'What a 'Racebent' Hermione Granger Really Represents'. *Buzzfeed*, 1 February. Available at: <www.buzzfeed.com/alannabennett/what-a-racebent-hermione-granger-really-represen-d2yp>.

Bennett, T. (1983). 'Text, Reader, Reading Formation'. *Literature and History*, 9(2).

Bird, S. E. (2003). *The Audience in Everyday Life: Living in a Media World*. Routledge.

Blumler, J. G. (1996). 'Recasting the Audience in the New Television Marketplace'. In: J. Hay, L. Grossberg & E. Wartella, eds. *The Audience and Its Landscape*. Westview Press, pp. 97–111.

Bly, R. (2004). *Iron John: A Book About Men*. Da Capo Press.

Bordwell, D., Staiger, J. & Thompson, K. (1985). *Classical Hollywood Cinema: Film Style and Mode of Production to 1960*. Columbia University Press.

Brennan, J., ed. (2019). *Queer Baiting and Fandom: Teasing Fans through Homoerotic Possibilities*. University of Iowa Press.

Brower, S. (1992). 'Fans as Tastemakers: Viewers for Quality Television'. In: L. Lewis, ed. *The Adoring Audience*. Taylor and Francis.

Brunk, K. H., Giesler, M. & Hartmann, B. J. (2018). 'Creating a Consumable Past: How Memory Making Shapes Marketization'. *Journal of Consumer Research*, 44(6), pp. 1325–1342.

Buccianti, A. (2010). 'Dubbed Turkish Soap Operas Conquering the Arab World: Social Liberation or Cultural Alienation'. *Arab Media and Society*, 10(2), pp. 428–442.

Campbell, John (2004). *Getting It On Online: Cyberspace, Gay Male Sexuality and Embodied Identity* (New York: Routledge).

Cavicchi, D. (2018). 'Foundational Discourses of Fandom'. In: P. Booth, ed. *A Companion to Media Fandom and Fan Studies*. Wiley Blackwell.

Chronis, A. (2008). 'Co-constructing the Narrative Experience: Staging and Consuming the American Civil War at Gettysburg'. *Journal of Marketing Management*, 24(1/2), pp. 5–27.

Coddington, M., Lewis, S. C. & Belair-Gagnon, V. (2021). 'The Imagined Audience for News: Where Does a Journalist's Perception of the Audience Come From?'. *Journalism Studies*, 22(8), pp. 1028–1046.

Couldry, N. (2010). *Why Voice Matters: Culture and Politics After Neoliberalism*. Sage.

Crenshaw, K. W. (2013). 'Mapping the Margins: Intersectionality, Identity Politics, and Violence Against Women of Color'. In: The Public Nature of Private Violence. Routledge, pp. 93–118.

Crotty, N. (2014). 'See Every Piece from CoverGirl's The Hunger Games: Catching Fire Capitol Collection'. *Fashionista*. Available at: https://fashionista.com/2013/09/see-every-piece-from-covergirls-the-hunger-games-catching-fire-capitol-collection.

Darnton, R. (1984). *The Great Cat Massacre and Other Episodes in French Cultural History*. Basic Books.

de Carvalho, A. P. M. & Frangella, R. de C. P. (2017). 'Here Comes Chavo! Everyone's Watching the TV: Thinking About Difference and Alterity, Childhood, and Education'. In: D. Friedrich & E. Colmenares, eds. *Resonances of El Chavo del Ocho in Latin American Childhood, Schooling, and Societies*. Bloomsbury, pp. 51–66.

Dyer, R. (1986). *Heavenly Bodies: Film Stars and Society*. Macmillan.

Eagle, R., Lander, R. & Hall, P. D. (2021). 'Questioning 'What Makes Us Human': How Audiences React to an Artificial Intelligence–Driven Show'. *Cognitive Computation and Systems*, 3(2), pp. 91–99.

Elkind, D. & Bowen, R. (1979). 'Imaginary Audience Behavior in Children and Adolescents'. *Developmental Psychology*, 15(1), pp. 38–44.

Fathallah, J. (2015). 'Moriarty's Ghost, Or the Queer Disruption of BBC's Sherlock'. *Television and New Media*, 16(5), pp. 490–500.

Fiske, J. & Hartley, J. (1978). *Reading Television*. Methuen.

Fiske, J. (1992). 'The Cultural Economy of Fandom'. In: L. A. Lewis, ed. *The Adoring Audience: Fan Culture and Popular Media*. Routledge.

Fish, S. (1982). *Is There a Text in This Class?: The Authority of Interpretive Communities*. Harvard University Press.

Flynn, P. (2019). *Superfans*. Get Smart Books.

Ford, S. (2018). '"He's A Real Man's Man': Pro Wrestling and Negotiations of Contemporary Masculinity'. In: M. A. Click & S. Scott, eds. *The Routledge Companion to Media Fandom*. Routledge.

Ford, S. (2019). 'The Marks Have Gone Off-Script: Rogue Actors on the WWE's Stands'. In: D. Jeffries, ed. *#WWE: World Wrestling Entertainment: Grappling with a Media Empire*. Indiana University Press, pp. 120–137.

Ford, S., De Kosnick, A. & Harrington, C. L., eds. (2010). *The Survival of Soap Operas: Transformations for a New Media Era*. University Press of Mississippi.

Foucault, M. (1999). 'What Is an Author.' In: J. D. Faubion, ed. *Aesthetics, Methods, and Epistemology*. The New Press.

Geertz, C. (1973). *The Interpretation of Cultures*. Basic Books.

Geertz, C. (1994). 'Deep Play: Notes on a Balinese Cock Fight.' In: A. Dundes, ed. *The Cock Fight: A Case Book*. University of Wisconsin Press.

Gerrig, R. J. (1993). *Experiencing Narrative Worlds: On the Psychological Activities of Reading*. Yale University Press.

Giddens, A. (1987). *Social Theory and Modern Sociology*. Stanford University Press.

Gilbert, A. (2019). 'Hatewatch with Me: Anti-fandom as Social Performance.' In: M. A. Click, ed. *Anti-Fandom: Dislike and Hate in the Digital Age*. New York University Press, pp. 62–80.

Grant, B. K. (2008). *Auteurs and Authorship: A Film Reader*. Wiley-Blackwell.

Gray, J. (2002). 'New Audiences, New Textualities: Anti-Fans and Non-Fans.' *International Journal of Cultural Studies*, 6(1), pp. 64–81.

Gray, J. (2010). *Show Sold Separately: Promos, Spoilers, and Other Media Paratexts*. New York University Press.

Gray, J. (2019). 'How Do I Dislike Thee? Let Me Count the Ways'. In: M. A. Click, ed. *Anti-Fandom: Dislike and Hate in the Digital Age*. New York University Press.

Griffith, C. R. (1921). 'A Comment Upon the Psychology of the Audience.' *Psychological Monographs*, 30(3), pp. 36–47.

Hailu, S. (2022). '"Wednesday' Production Designer Explains Inspiration and Process Behind the Stained Glass, Romanian Forest and Shrunken Head'. *Variety*. Available at: https://variety.com/2022/artisans/news/wednesday-production-designer-stained-glass-1235440848.

Hall, S. (1980). 'Encoding/Decoding'. In: S. Hall et al., eds. *Culture, Media, Language*. Hutchinson, pp. 134–148.

Hall, S. (1981). 'Notes on Deconstructing 'The Popular''. In: J. Storey, ed. *Cultural Theory and Popular Culture: A Reader*. Routledge, pp. 508–518.

Hall, S. (1983). *Cultural Studies 1983: A Theoretical History*. Duke University Press.

Hall, S. (1992). 'What is This 'Black' in Black Popular Culture?'. In: M. Wallace & G. Dent, eds. *Black Popular Culture: A Project*. Bay Press, pp. 21–33.

Hartley, J. (1992). *Studies in Television*. Routledge.

Hills, M. (2023). 'Martin Barker's Work in Relation to Fan Studies and Fans: On 'Rogue' Readings, 'Figures of the Audience,' and 'Waves' of Scholarship'. *Participations*. Available at: https://www.participations.org/19-03-05-hills.pdf.

Hobson, D. (1982). *Crossroads: The Drama of a Soap Opera*. Methuen.

Hollebeek, L. D., Glynn, M. S. & Brodie, R. J. (2014). 'Consumer Brand Engagement in Social Media: Conceptualization, Scale Development and Validation.' *Journal of Interactive Marketing*, 28(2), pp. 149–165.

Horak, R. (2006). 'Wir müssen den Leuten endlich das marktwirtschaftliche Denken in die Köpfe pflanzen!: Über Universitätsreform und prekäre Intellektuelle in Österreich.' In: Kongress der Deutschen Gesellschaft für Soziologie, ed. *Soziale Ungleichheit-kulturelle Unterschiede*. Campus Verl, pp. 4283–4291.

Hua, J. (2009). "Gucci Geishas' and Post-Feminism'. *Women's Studies in Communication*, 32(1), pp. 63–88.

Hyslop, J. (2013). "'Days of Miracle and Wonder'? Conformity and Revolt in Searching for Sugar Man," *Safundi*, 14(4), pp. 490–501.

IGN (2016, April 25). *Telltale's The Walking Dead - Robert Kirkman Interview* [Video]. Available at: https://www.youtube.com/watch?v=5JP1qKlPuMM.

Jenkins III, H. (1988). 'Star Trek Rerun, Reread, Rewritten: Fan Writing as Textual Poaching.' *Critical Studies in Media Communication*, 5(2), pp. 85–107.

Jenkins, H. (1992). *Textual Poachers: Television Fans and Participatory Culture*. Routledge.

Jenkins, H. (1995). "'Do You Enjoy Making the Rest of Us Feel Stupid?': alt. tv.twinpeaks, the Trickster Author and Viewer Mastery," In: D. Lavery, ed. *Full of Secrets: Critical Approaches to Twin Peaks*. Wayne State University Press.

Jenkins, H. (2000). 'Reception Theory and Audience Research: The Mystery of the Vampire's Kiss.' In: C. Gledhill & L. Williams, eds. *Reinventing Film Studies*. Arnold, pp. 165–182.

Jenkins, H. (2007). *The Wow Climax: Tracing the Emotional Impact of Popular Culture*. New York University Press.

Jenkins, H. (2008). *Convergence Culture: Where Old and New Media Collide*. New York University Press.

Jenkins, H. (2010). 'The Hollywood Geek Elite Debates the Future of Television'. *Pop Junctions* (previously Confessions of an Aca-Fan), June 2. http://henryjenkins.org/blog/2010/06/the_hollywood_geek_elite_debat.html?rq=Lost.

Jenkins, H. (2012). 'The Guiding Spirit and the Powers That Be: A Response to Suzanne Scott', in Delwiche, A. and Henderson, J.J. (eds.) *The Participatory Cultures Handbook*. Routledge, pp. 53-58.

Jenkins, H. (2013). 'Reading Critically and Reading Creatively', in Jenkins, H., Kelly, W., Clinton, K.A., McWilliams, J., Pitts-Wiley, R. and Reilly, E. (eds.) *Reading in a Participatory Culture: Remixing Moby-Dick in the Literature Classroom*. Teachers College Press.

Jenkins, H. (2013). 'Same Old Shit: Fan Resistance at Wrestlemania 29', *Pop Junctions* (formerly *Confessions of an Aca-Fan*), 16 April.

Jenkins, H. (2014). 'The Reign of the "Mothership": Transmedia's Past, Present, and Possible Futures', in Mann, D. (ed.) *Wired TV: Laboring Over an Interactive Future*. Rutgers University Press, pp. 244-268.

Jenkins, H. (2016a). 'Henry Jenkins on John Fiske', in Hobbs, R. (ed.) *Exploring the Roots of Digital and Media Literacy Through Personal Narrative*. Temple University Press, pp. 138-152.

Jenkins, H. (2016b). 'Transmedia Logics and Locations', in Kurtz, B.W.L.D. and Bourdaa, M. (eds.) *The Rise of the Transtexts: Challenges and Opportunities*. Routledge, pp. 220-240.

Jenkins, H. (2017). 'Negotiating Fandom: The Politics of Race-Bending', in Click, M.A. and Scott, S. (eds.) *The Routledge Companion of Fandom Studies*. Routledge.

Jenkins, H. (2025). 'Transmedia Tarantino: Reading the Many Texts of Once Upon a Time in Hollywood', in Gray, J. (ed.) *Reading Media: New Horizons in Textual Analysis*. New York University Press.

Jenkins, H., Ford, S. and Green, J. (2013). *Spreadable Media: Creating Meaning and Value in a Networked Culture*. New York University Press.

Jenkins, H. and Jenkins, C. (2021). 'Static Cling', in Braccia, N. (ed.) *Off the Back of the Truck: Unofficial Contraband for the Survivor Fan*. Simon Element.

Jenkins, H. and Tulloch, J. (1994). *Science Fiction Audiences: Watching Star Trek and Doctor Who*. Routledge.

Jones, B. (2023). *Forensic Fandom: True Crime, Citizen Investigation, and Social Media*. London: Routledge.

Kasson, J.F. (1990). *Rudeness and Civility: Manners in Nineteenth-Century America*. Hill and Wang.

Kaufmann, V. (2006). *Guy Debord: Revolution in the Service of Poetry*, trans. Bononno, R. University of Minnesota Press.

Kozinets, R.V. (2001). 'Utopian Enterprise: Articulating the Meanings of Star Trek's Culture of Consumption', *Journal of Consumer Research*, 28(1), pp. 67-88.

Larkin, B. (1997). 'Indian Films and Nigerian Lovers: Media and the Creation of Parallel Modernities', *Africa*, 67(3).

Levy, P. (1997). *Collective Intelligence: Mankind's Emerging World in Cyberspace* (New York: Plenium).

Liebes, T. and Katz, E. (1990). *The Export of Meaning: Cross-Cultural Readings of Dallas*. Oxford University Press.

Lipsitz, G. (1997). *Dangerous Crossroads: Popular Music, Postmodernism and the Poetics of Place*. Verso.

Litherland, B. (2014). 'Breaking Kayfabe is Easy, Cheap and Never Entertaining: Twitter Rivalries in Professional Wrestling', *Celebrity Studies*, 5(4), pp. 531-533.

Litt, E. (2012). 'Knock, Knock. Who's There? The Imagined Audience', *Journal of Broadcasting & Electronic Media*, 56(3), pp. 330-345.

Martin, A.L. (2021). 'Surplus Blackness', *Flow*, 27 April. Available at: https://www.flowjournal.org/2021/04/surplus-blackness/.

Mittell, J. (2016). 'Forensic Fandom and the Drillable Text', *Spreadable Media*. Available at: https://spreadablemedia.org/essays/mittell/index.html.

Mittell, J. (2008). 'All in the Game: The Wire, Serial Storytelling and Procedural Logic', in Harrigan, P. and Wardip-Fruin, N. (eds.) *Third Person*. MIT Press.

Morley, D. (1980). *The Nationwide Audience: Structure and Decoding*. British Film Institute.

Pearce, C., Boellstorff, T. and Nardi, B.A. (2009). *Communities of Play: Emergent Cultures in Multiplayer Games and Virtual Worlds*. MIT Press.

Philosophistry (2013). 'Hate Watching'. Available at: https://www.urbandictionary.com/define.php?term=hate%20watching.

Postman, N. (1985). *Amusing Ourselves to Death: Public Discourse in the Age of Show Business*. Viking.

Proctor, W. (2020). 'Rebel Yell: The Metapolitics of Equality and Diversity in Disney's Star Wars', in Jenkins, H., Peters-Lazzaro, G. and Shresthova, S. (eds.) *Popular Culture and the Civic Imagination: Case Studies of Creative Social Change*. New York University Press, pp. 35-42.

Radway, J. (1984). *Reading the Romance: Women, Patriarchy and Popular Literature*. University of North Carolina Press.

Rabinowitz, P.J. (1985). 'The Turn Turn of the Glass Key: Popular Fiction as Reading Strategy', *Critical Inquiry*, 11(3).

Reed, K. (2024). 'Fifty Shades of Fandom: Black Women, Shame, and the Changing Same of Fanfiction', PhD Dissertation, University of Southern California.

Reyes, Y.M. (2024). 'Culture as a Constitutive Dimension of Social Life: Theoretical Proposals of Raymond Williams and Clifford Geertz. Convergences and Divergences', *Southern Perspective/Perspectiva Austral*, 2, p. 57.

Rosaldo, R. (1993). *Culture and Truth: The Remaking of Social Analysis*. Beacon Press.

Russell, C.A., Norman, A.T. and Heckler, S.E. (2004). 'The Consumption of Television Programming: Development and Validation of the Connectedness Scale', *Journal of Consumer Research*, 31(1), pp. 150-161.

Sarin, S. (2010). 'Market Segmentation and Targeting', *Wiley International Encyclopedia of Marketing*.

Shannon, C. and Weaver, W. (1948). 'The Mathematical Theory of Communication', *Bell System Technical Journal*, 27, pp. 379-423.

Shresthova, Sangita (2025). "Imagining through Appropriation: Exploring Contested Migrations of Bollywood Dance," unpublished manuscript.

Starz (2014). 'Ronald D. Moore shares his "Outlander" strategy.' Available at: https://www.youtube.com/watch?v=TApo_3Yql9A

Thomas, E.E. (2019). *The Dark Fantastic: Race and the Imagination from Harry Potter to The Hunger Games*. New York University Press.

Tulloch, J. and Alvarado, M. (1983). *Doctor Who: The Unfolding Text*. St. Martin's Press.

Tulloch, J. and Jenkins, H. (1995). *Science Fiction Audiences: Watching Doctor Who and Star Trek*. Routledge.

Tulloch, J. (2000). *Watching Television Audiences: Cultural Theories and Methods*. Arnold.

Tulloch, J. (2007). 'Chekhov's fans: Re-approaching "high culture"', in Gray, J., Sandvoss, C. and Harrington, L. (eds.) *Fandom: Identities and Communities in a Mediated World*. New York University Press, pp. 110–122.

Van Laer, T., De Ruyter, K., Visconti, L.M. and Wetzels, M. (2014). 'The extended transportation-imagery model: A meta-analysis of the antecedents and consequences of consumers' narrative transportation,' *Journal of Consumer Research*, 40(5), pp. 797–817.

Webster, J.G. (1998). 'The audience,' *Journal of Broadcasting & Electronic Media*, 42(2), pp. 190–207.

Williams, R. (1989). "Culture is ordinary," in *Resources of Hope: Culture, Democracy, Socialism*, London: Verso, pp. 3-14.

Williams, R. (1976). 'Culture,' in *Keywords: A Vocabulary of Culture and Society*. London: Croom Helm, pp. 87–93.

Williams, R. (2020). *Theme Park Fandom: Spatial Transmedia, Materiality and Participatory Cultures*. Amsterdam University Press.

INDEX

www.ingramcontent.com/pod-product-compliance
Lightning Source LLC
Chambersburg PA
CBHW072127270326
41931CB00010B/1696